Merry Christmas - 97
John & Mary

**TEXAS TORTES**

To Anne,

Enjoy!

Art Meyer
5/3/97

*Illustrations by John A. Wilson*

UNIVERSITY OF TEXAS PRESS, AUSTIN

# ·TEXAS·

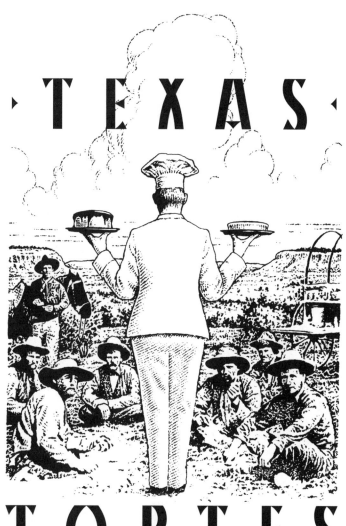

# TORTES

## A Collection of Recipes
## from the Heart of Texas

### Arthur L. Meyer

♾The paper used in this publication meets the minimum
requirements of American National Standard for Infor-
mation Sciences—Permanence of Paper for Printed Library Materials, ANSI Z39.48–1984.

Library of Congress Cataloging-in-Publication Data

Meyer, Arthur L.
    Texas tortes / by Arthur L. Meyer.
        p.   cm.
    Includes index.
    ISBN 0-292-75201-6 (alk. paper).
    1. Desserts.   2. Cookery—Texas.   I. Title.
    TX773.M48   1997
    641.8′6—dc20                                    96–9422

*This book is dedicated to the memory of Belle Meyer, whose love, selfless devotion, and lasting guidance made this endeavor possible.*

# Contents

## Basics

## Fruit Tortes

## Nut Tortes

## Chocolate Tortes

## Cassate

## Tarts and Pies

## Cheesecakes

## Other Desserts

# Foreword

This book contains a wonderful collection of European-style desserts. Art Meyer's philosophy of adapting classic European recipes to fit in with Texans' tastes and appetites is very much in line with my experience. As the owner of Alain and Marie LeNôtre Bakeries, I have brought classic French pastry to Texas as well as to Germany and Japan. I especially like the way Art has incorporated local Texas produce into his recipes. Being from France, I grew up with local markets; fresh natural ingredients were used at home as well as in fine restaurants and bakeries. The recipes in this book should appeal to a wide audience, as they fit into traditional cake categories. While not for the beginner, the recipes are easy to follow and reflect Art's extensive experience as a master baker. It is clear that these recipes have been directly adapted from his bakery and thoroughly tested. Art provides careful directions, observations, and hints; his "Getting Started" section should be particularly helpful to the home baker.

I became acquainted with Art Meyer and his vast knowledge of professional baking while trying to find someone who could help with some highly technical challenges I was facing in formulating high-quality specialty desserts to be manufactured on a larger-than-usual scale. Being located in Houston, I cannot always find the time to travel to Austin to solve problems that sometimes arise with a facility I use to subcontract with a large retailer. I asked a pastry chef of my acquaintance who now owns two French bakeries in Austin to find someone with enough experience to fill in for me. My former associate told me that I was lucky because the perfect person for the job was in Austin. He was a talented and resourceful pastry chef who was also a chemistry professor at the university. (Interestingly, a bakery kitchen in France is known as a laboratory.) Art and I began a business relationship in which he was able to use his unique problem-solving skills related to bakery manufacturing as well as his all-around talent in baking. To this day, whenever Alain and Marie LeNôtre Bakeries starts a new project, I know that I can rely on Art to give accurate, thoroughly researched opinions regarding any aspect of baking that will help to maintain our bakery's excellent reputation for quality and consistency.

For maximum enjoyment of Art Meyer's collection of carefully thought-out recipes, I recommend that you include your children and friends in family baking projects. I know that Art loves to have children in his kitchen (the annual Christmas cookie party at his bakery is legendary) and my son Gaston, who is twelve, loves wearing an apron and chef's hat while mixing ingredients. The joy in their eyes when seeing the magic that comes from the oven is only heightened by the pleasures of tasting and in sharing. Bon appetit!

—Alain LeNôtre

# Introduction

◇

The image of Texas that most readily comes to mind is that of mesas and buttes, right out of Hollywood's classic portrayal of the West. While it is true that Texas has its share of desert expanse and traditional cowboy settings, it is equally true that Texans grow some of the finest oranges in the United States as well as some of the juiciest and most flavorful peaches. Pecans, raspberries, blueberries, plums, apricots, figs, kiwis, and strawberries are all grown in Texas. Countless varieties of honey are produced across the state. Citrus from the Rio Grande Valley and raisins from Gardendale make wonderful additions to desserts. Canyon, Denton, and San Antonio produce high-quality baking flours, and Austin is home to America's favorite producer of flavorings and extracts.

Fresh ingredients are a must when it comes to creating great desserts, and using locally grown produce means that the fruit can be ripened on the plant, picked at the height of flavor, and delivered to markets the same day. Owing to modern distribution systems, markets all over the United States are stocked with "fresh" produce from around the world. Always seek out those items that are grown locally and are in season.

My philosophy behind preparing foods of the highest quality is simple. Use the very best ingredients, apply basic techniques which rely on fundamental principles, and allow the ingredients to show through.

Texas tortes are adaptations of classic European desserts. Of course, you don't have to be a Texan or live in Texas to make the desserts in this book. Most of the ingredients are not unique to Texas, but—surprisingly even to some native Texans—this great state does produce many of the fruits and other ingredients necessary for such specialty cakes and other treats. I have adjusted these recipes to suit local and American tastes. Many of us, for example, perceive nut tortes made without flour as in Vienna to be too dry, with a bit too much "texture." Replacing some of the ground nuts with flour and adding additional liquid brings the *Texas Tortes* version more in line with American expectations. Like their European counterparts, Texas tortes are quite rich and not particularly sweet. Chocolate flavors tend to be on the bitter side; and buttercreams, dominated by their flavorings and silky texture, are never granular or sugary.

Many of the desserts in this book rely on basic recipes, which are found in the first chapter. In most instances, do not attempt to do everything on the day you want to serve the dessert. Although the recipes are sequenced as though the steps would all be completed in the same time frame, many of the components can be made ahead, reducing the stress and anxiety associated with complex recipes. In addition, many of the desserts benefit from a day or so of resting, which allows the flavors to "marry." As a matter of fact, these desserts "hold" very well, so don't be afraid of making a large cake and having leftovers for several days. If wrapped properly, any remaining cake can be frozen and enjoyed at a later date, but don't be surprised if you find your dessert all gone by morning, the result of several midnight raids on the "fridge."

# Getting Started

To get consistent, satisfactory results, some basic techniques should be followed. They relate to organization and preparation, measurement, and proper application of heat when baking. The most important lesson that I've learned about life is to enjoy the process of a task rather than to expect the finished product to be the reward. I believe this is especially true for baking, and being organized will greatly enhance your enjoyment of the creative process of producing fine desserts. Make lists! Shop early and completely. Assemble all of the ingredients and have everything measured out in advance, as good Chinese chefs do. They do not have time to stop and chop a vegetable once they start the chowing process, and you shouldn't have to stop to separate the eggs while the batter is mixing. The same is true for the equipment and utensils that you'll be using. Don't wait until you need the spatula to start looking for it. Read through the recipe and set everything out in a logical place. Pan preparation falls into this category as well. Once the batter is done you shouldn't have to stop and line a pan with parchment (or find it for that matter).

And speaking of preparation, be sure to have a look at Appendixes I and II on such techniques as frosting and decorating, pan preparation, torting layers, fruit preparation, and so forth. Like the basic recipes, these are designed to give you more flexibility in creating your own recipes as well as to amplify techniques that are used throughout the book. These appendixes are cross-referenced from the recipes where relevant.

Advance preparation includes your oven. Always preheat the oven at least one hour before using it. Proper application of heat starts with a properly calibrated oven. Do not trust the numbers on your oven dial, which can be off by as much as 75 degrees; use a good oven thermometer. If oven temperatures vary with time, you may need a new thermostat. Remember . . . the oven is the heart of baking. It doesn't matter how good the pans are or how expensive the ingredients, your cake will burn or come out "raw" if the oven is not working properly.

You can get more even heating by using the following tricks. First, I never try to bake on more than one level, as this plays havoc with heat distribution and circulation. Remove all but one of the wire shelves from the oven. Second, I cover the surface of the shelf with quarry tiles (ceramic floor tiles). This allows for even distribution of heat to the bottom of the pans and keeps the temperature more consistent. Commercial deck ovens have thick stone bases on which the pans are placed; at my bakery the stones were two inches thick and weighed about two hundred pounds.

Another very important rule of successful baking is to make accurate measurements. Unlike most types of cooking, baking requires precise ratios for proper results. Professional bakers rarely use volume measurements but weigh their ingredients out on scales. Try to use a good scale whenever an ingredient is specified by weight, e.g., 12 ounces bittersweet chocolate. When measuring by volume, be aware of the difference between dry and liquid measures. Have a set of dry measuring cups for flour and sugar, and don't estimate. If the recipe calls for one-half cup of sugar, don't fill a one cup measure about halfway. Use a one-half cup measure, fill it, and pass a straight edge across the top to even it. Use graduated measuring cups for liquids. A complete list of recommended equipment and tools for producing the desserts in this book is provided in Appendix III, but don't be intimidated by it. Don't rush out to buy everything before trying a recipe. Adapt, if necessary. A tart made in a pie pan will taste every bit as good as one made in a specialty tart pan! I do feel, however, that a quality electric mixer is essential in producing consistent results. Necessary attachments include only the flat beater (paddle) and whip.

Finally, be innovative. Use the basic recipes given at the beginning of the book to create your own cakes and tortes. Make a raspberry buttercream and combine it with a chocolate cake. Use the lemon filling from the lemon almond tart as a filling for a genoise cake. Make the pavé with a passion fruit buttercream and fill it with fresh papaya! Above all, enjoy the process of making the desserts and the reward of pleasing others with your creations.

Oh . . . and don't forget to cut a large slice for the baker.

# ► BASICS ◄

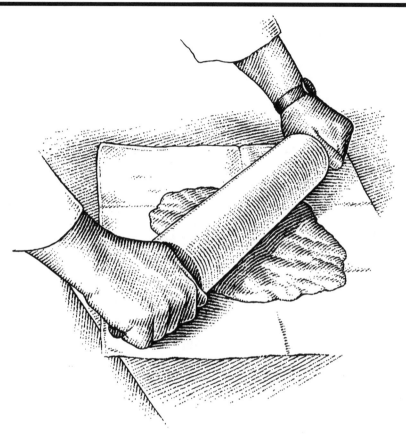

# Pâté Brisé

Pâté brisé is a French pie dough with one important difference from most American pie crusts. It's an all-butter crust, so the flavor is especially delicate, and it is almost moisture proof. This is a useful feature with savory dishes such as quiche, in which large amounts of liquids are used. If you hate a soggy crust in your pies, use this dough. You will sacrifice some tenderness, as the dough is a bit firm, but it stays crisp for days and can tolerate extremely moist fillings (fruit pie fillings, custards, etc.). A problem to consider when baking this crust "blind" (without filling) is that it will shrink. I've developed a technique that yields perfect results, however. I bake the crust upside down, with another pie pan inside the formed dough. This recipe will make a double crust. It expands well for holiday baking (at my bakery I've expanded it fivefold easily, with excellent results).

*3 cups all-purpose flour*
*6 ounces unsalted butter, chilled thoroughly*
*6 to 8 tablespoons ice water*

1.   Measure the flour into a large bowl.
2.   Cut the butter into pieces and toss with the flour. With cold hands press the pieces to flatten them in the flour.
3.   Using a pastry knife, cut the butter into the flour to form very small pieces of butter in the flour, approximating the consistency of rolled oats.
4.   Add six tablespoons of the ice water and mix quickly to form a dough. Add additional water in small amounts as necessary to form a ball. Use as little water as possible for best results.
5.   Divide the dough in half. Flatten each piece between two pieces of plastic wrap and "streak" the dough with the heel of your hand, spreading it from the center out into an elongated oval. You should observe streaks of butter throughout the dough. Wrap the dough in the plastic and refrigerate at least thirty minutes.

# Tart Dough

This is an excellent all-purpose dough to use for filled tarts as well as when baking "blind." The recipe yields a double crust and freezes well.

*8 ounces unsalted butter, at room temperature*

*1 cup sugar*

*3 eggs*

*3 cups all-purpose flour*

1.   Take butter out of refrigerator at least thirty minutes before beginning recipe.

2.   With the electric mixer, cream the butter with the sugar until fluffy and smooth, about two minutes. Add the eggs, one at a time, scraping down the bowl between eggs. Beat one minute.

3.   With the mixer on low speed, stir in the flour. Scrape down the bowl and stir briefly to form a dough.

4.   Wrap in plastic and refrigerate several hours, until firm. This dough freezes well.

# Cheesecake Crust Dough

A proper crust for a cheesecake should be a baked dough. This recipe is an adaptation from Mrs. Petrocelli's "walnut ricotta chocolate chip cookies" (she was a neighbor and the perfect Italian grandmother . . . always dressed in black and so round that it was impossible to lock your hands around her when hugging). Needless to say, leftover dough makes terrific cookies. I used to make *mezzalunas* (half-moons) for a restaurant staff on Fridays by forming leftover dough into rounds, placing a vertical crease in each with the back of a knife, and dipping them halfway in chocolate after baking. This recipe will make two crusts or one crust plus enough dough for a fair-sized batch of cookies. Add chocolate chips, nuts, or whatever you like.

*4 ounces unsalted butter*

*1/4 cup ricotta cheese*

*1 teaspoon vanilla extract*

*1 cup sugar*

*1 egg*

*2 cups all-purpose flour*

*1 teaspoon baking powder*

1.    Combine the butter, ricotta, vanilla, and sugar in a mixing bowl and cream with the electric mixer until the mixture becomes fluffy and the sugar dissolves, about three minutes. Add the egg, scrape down the bowl, and mix thirty seconds more.

2.    Sift the flour with the baking powder and add it to the bowl. With the mixer on low speed, stir to incorporate, forming a smooth dough. Wrap in plastic and refrigerate one hour before use. This dough will hold for several days in the refrigerator or can be frozen.

# Genoise

Genoise is a butter sponge cake—rich yet light, and very tasty. It goes especially well with fruit, custards, and chocolate, of course. This batter is also used to make the famous madeleine, a French cookie baked in a shell mold. It may be the most mispronounced cake in the industry, usually mutilated as "jen-WAH." One of my favorite bakery delivery stories centers around the delivery of cassata (which uses genoise) to a rather prestigious restaurant. The chef asked, as I was placing cassate in the walk-in refrigerator, "When will the jen-WAH fall?". I couldn't help saying "The jen-wahz is a cake, not a soufflé."

> *8 eggs*
> *1 cup sugar*
> *1 tablespoon vanilla extract*
> *1 1/2 cups all-purpose flour*
> *4 ounces unsalted butter, melted and cooled*

1. Place the eggs in a large bowl in the sink and run warm water over them for a few minutes to ensure that they are at the proper temperature. They must be warm to attain proper volume: the air beaten into the eggs is the sole leavening agent.
2. Beat the eggs with the sugar and vanilla at high speed for five minutes or so, until maximum volume is observed (the mixture will no longer creep up the sides of the bowl).
3. Gently fold in the flour by hand.
4. Melt butter and stir in with the mixer on low speed.
5. Bake as directed in the specific cake recipes that call for genoise.

# Chocolate Genoise

Substitute 1/2 cup of cocoa powder for an equal amount of flour in the basic recipe.

# Basic Chocolate Cake

There are hundreds of recipes for chocolate cakes. I wanted one recipe that could be counted on to never fail and to have the following properties: a pronounced chocolate flavor, fine crumb, delicate texture, and just the right moisture content. This cake is it (it's like June Cleaver, Christie Brinkley, and Madame Curie rolled into one). It is not a one-step, mix-it-all-together recipe, but the results are well worth the effort.

*6 eggs*

*1 3/4 cups sugar*

*8 ounces butter*

*8 ounces bittersweet chocolate, chopped fine*

*1/3 cup milk*

*2/3 cup heavy cream*

*1 1/2 cups all-purpose flour*

*1/4 cup cocoa powder*

*2 teaspoons baking powder*

1.   Separate the eggs. Whip the whites with 3/4 cup of the sugar in an electric mixer to form firm peaks. Do not overbeat them. Set aside.

2.   Using an electric mixer, cream the butter with the remaining sugar. While this is mixing, scald the milk, then pour the hot milk over the chocolate to melt it. If some of the chocolate remains unmelted, carefully microwave on low or heat over simmering water in a double boiler until melted. Stir the chocolate mixture until it is smooth.

3.   Add the egg yolks to the butter mixture. Beat until smooth. Scrape down the sides of the bowl and beat two minutes more.

4.   Add the chocolate mixture and stir in until smooth. Scrape down the sides of the bowl and add the cream. Beat for one minute.

5.   Sift the dry ingredients together and add to the batter, stirring carefully. Scrape down the bowl and mix thirty seconds.

6.   Gently fold in the egg whites until the batter is uniform in texture.

7.   Bake as directed.

# Buttercream Base

This is the true buttercream. Beware of recipes found in some cake decorating books that have you beat butter into a Crisco/powdered sugar base; these products leave an unpleasant coating in your mouth. This recipe is very, very rich but has a satiny texture and a spectacular taste. It will accept a variety of flavorings, from fruit purees and chocolates to extracts and liqueurs. It pipes well from a pastry bag but is extremely sensitive to heat. A local "good foods" market wanted to carry one of my bakery's tortes and called in a small order. When I arrived I started searching for their refrigerated display cabinet, but saw none. I asked the bakery manager about this and was told that they didn't have one but felt it would be all right to leave the torte out. I explained that it had a buttercream frosting that would not do well in the ambient conditions of a Texas summer. But a sale is a sale. I went back three hours later to check on the cake. It looked like an idea for Stephen King's next book, *The Children's Cake*. I bought the entire cake (at retail price) and threw it in the trash.

Read Appendix I on frosting and decorating before applying frosting.

> 1/3 cup water
> 1 cup sugar
> 6 egg yolks
> 3/4 pound unsalted butter, at room temperature (soft)
> 1/2 tablespoon vanilla extract

1. Remove butter from refrigerator at least thirty minutes before you will need it.
2. Add the sugar to the water in a heavy saucepan. Heat to boiling. Continue to boil, without stirring, until the syrup takes on a slight color and is at the "large pearl" stage (slow, large bubbles forming in the syrup).
3. While the syrup is developing, beat the egg yolks thoroughly until pale yellow and thick.

**4**. As soon as the syrup is ready, add it, a little at a time to the egg yolks while continuing to beat them. Be careful! The syrup is extremely hot and should not be allowed to hit the moving beater. When all of the syrup has been added, beat the mixture thoroughly until cool to the touch.

**5**.    Add the butter in quarters to the cool egg mixture. Scrape down the bowl and beat thirty seconds. Add the vanilla, scrape the bowl and beat thirty seconds more. The buttercream should be smooth and silky. Use immediately or refrigerate, wrapped in plastic. If refrigerated, allow it to come to room temperature before using.

A note about flavorings: While I've given a few ideas for buttercream flavorings in this book, almost any fruit-flavored buttercream can be made. Preserves make a good flavoring additive, combined with a little lemon juice. Purees are excellent, as well. Some that we have tried successfully at Texas Tortes Bakery include plum, apricot, raspberry, strawberry, currant, blueberry, pineapple, passion fruit, peach, and blackberry.

Extracts such as spearmint and peppermint make delicious flavored buttercreams as well as coffee, vanilla, lemon, and rum. Chocolates such as milk, bittersweet, white, and hazelnut are excellent as well.

▼

# Chocolate Base

◇

For the life of me I couldn't come up with a better name for this product. It can be used as a frosting as is. It makes a great truffle when bittersweet chocolate is added. When heated it makes a fabulous glaze, remaining shiny when cool. It can be added to buttercream or ricotta filling for flavoring. Let me know if you have a better name and I'll use it.

Read Appendix I on frosting and decorating before applying frosting.

◇

*2 cups heavy cream*

*2 cups sugar*

*4 ounces unsalted butter*

*2 cups cocoa powder (22 – 24 percent butterfat)*

1.  Place the cream in a heavy saucepan. Add the sugar and heat to boiling, stirring occasionally.

2.  Add the butter and stir to dissolve. Make sure the butter has been incorporated into the mixture.

3.  Place the hot cream mixture into a mixing bowl, add the cocoa, and whip on medium speed for three minutes or so. Scrape down the bowl and continue to mix until cool.

4.  Package in plastic containers and refrigerate until needed. This product holds very well in the refrigerator for several weeks.

▼

# Chocolate Ganache

◇

Ganache is a cross between frosting and whipped cream. It's firm, yet light. Beware of recipes that turn out a dense, chocolatey fudge frosting, as they are, in fact, fudge frostings rather than ganache. Prepare it as you would whipped cream, being careful not to overbeat it, as it will curdle. While working in the bakery one morning, I heard a radio ad from a local restaurant/bakery describing one of their wonderful desserts, topped with *grenache*. I called and asked them for their secret in preventing the grenache (a cheap wine) from running off or soaking into the cake. They hadn't a clue.

Read Appendix I on frosting and decorating before applying frosting.

◇

*2 cups heavy cream*

*10 ounces bittersweet chocolate*

1. Scald the cream in a heavy saucepan or in the microwave.
2. Break up the chocolate into a bowl and pour the hot cream over it. Allow it to stand for a few minutes, then stir with a rubber spatula to form a smooth mixture. Chill thoroughly, preferably overnight.
3. Whip the chilled mixture until stiff, folding once or twice. Do not overbeat. Use immediately or refrigerate.
4. A variety of flavors may be added just before chilling, such as concentrated orange juice, raspberry liqueur, coffee, or other flavoring.

# Old-Fashioned Chocolate Frosting

This is the frosting originally developed for my *Extra-Fat Chocolate Cake*, a fifties-style, fudgey chocolate cake. It is simple to prepare and irresistible to sample directly from the bowl, bypassing the cake completely.

Read Appendix I on frosting and decorating before applying frosting.

◇

*10 ounces sour cream, at room temperature*

*1 cup sugar*

*1 teaspoon vanilla extract, orange liqueur, or other flavoring*

*1 pound bittersweet chocolate*

1. Remove sour cream from refrigerator thirty minutes before it will be used.
2. Beat the sugar with the sour cream in an electric mixer until the sugar is dissolved, about three minutes. Add the flavoring of your choice and mix one minute more.
3. Melt the chocolate in a microwave oven at low power or in the top of a double boiler over simmering water. Do not overheat the chocolate; it should be just melted.

**4.** Add the chocolate to the sour cream mixture and beat until uniform. Scrape down the bowl and beat thirty seconds. Place it over a bowl of warm water if it gets too firm to spread.

# Crispy Pecans

This recipe is included here because (1) it is a time-consuming step in the single recipe in this book that uses it and (2) its product is a delicious confection. This recipe can be doubled or tripled quite successfully, and if you are going to make the Native Pecan Praline Torte, it would make sense to increase the yield from one cup to two or three, utilizing the extra pecans as gifts, treats, and so forth.

*1 cup pecans*
*2 cups sugar*
*1 cup water*

**I.** Shell pecans if necessary, being careful to remove any small bits of shell or membrane.

**2.** Prepare a simple syrup by adding the sugar to the water in a heavy saucepan, and allow to boil without stirring. Add the cup of whole pecans to the syrup and continue to boil for thirty to forty minutes, or until the pecans are cooked through and sweet to taste. Be very careful not to burn the pecans during this operation. Drain them thoroughly. Save the syrup for step 9 in the Native Pecan Praline Torte recipe, or use it on pancakes if you're only preparing the pecans.

**3.** Deep-fry the drained pecans in oil at 375°F until dark, but not burned. Spread them out on a sheet pan, not touching, to cool. They should have a deep color with a lacquered look to them.

# ▸ FRUIT TORTES ◂

- Blueberry Lemon Yogurt Cake

- Strawberry Mango Charlotte Russe Cake

- Babba's Apple Cake

- Hill Country Peach Pavé

- Apple Walnut Torte

- Banana Chocolate Chip Cake

# Blueberry Lemon Yogurt Cake

I was known in my family as the "blueberry kid." Whenever we ate out, usually at a diner, I would order blueberry pie, whether it was on the menu or not. I would pick wild blueberries whenever the opportunity arose to coax my mother into baking a pie. For a meatless meal we would have "berries and cream" if it was too hot in the kitchen to cook. Keeping this in mind, imagine my pleasure when I discovered that Texas grew giant blueberries. Big Blues®, as they are known, are grown near the Texas towns of Hooks, Livingston, and Rusk, and Georgetown is home to the Texas Blueberry Marketing Association. The name of this cake might give the impression that it is a light, fruity dessert. It is not. It is a very rich and dense, torte-style cake owing much of its richness to the ground almonds in the batter.

*1/2 pound unsalted butter at room temperature*
*2 cups sugar*
*4 eggs*
*1 teaspoon vanilla extract*
*1 tablespoon lemon zest*
*1/2 cup lemon juice, freshly squeezed*
*1 cup plain yogurt*
*2 1/2 cups all-purpose flour*
*1 cup ground almonds*
*1 teaspoon baking soda*
*1 teaspoon baking powder*
*1 pint blueberries*
*1 recipe Buttercream Base (see basic recipes)*

1.   Take the butter from the refrigerator at least thirty minutes before it will be needed.
2.   Preheat the oven to 350°F.
3.   Prepare two round parchment-lined 9-inch cake pans (see Appendix II–1).

**4.**   Cream the butter and the sugar together with an electric mixer for two or three minutes until pale and fluffy.

**5.**   With the mixer running, add the eggs, one at a time. Scrape down the bowl and mix one minute more.

**6.**   Add the vanilla, zest, all but one tablespoon of the lemon juice, and yogurt. Mix to blend. Scrape down the bowl and mix one minute.

**7.**   Combine the remaining dry ingredients, add them to the mixture in the bowl and, with the mixer on low speed, gently stir to incorporate.

**8.**   Gently fold in one cup of the blueberries.

**9.**   Divide the batter between the two parchment-lined cake pans. Bake until golden and firm to the touch in the center, about thirty minutes. Allow to cool.

**10.**   Puree the remaining blueberries and press them through a fine wire mesh sieve to remove skins and seeds, using a rubber spatula or the back of a spoon. Beat this puree into the buttercream. Taste the frosting and add 1 tablespoon lemon juice if desired.

**11.**   Fill the cake layers with blueberry buttercream, then use it to frost the cake, forming pronounced peaks with your spatula by pulling up on the frosting as you apply it.

# Strawberry Mango Charlotte Russe Cake

◇

It's not quite tropical enough in Texas to grow mangos, but they are quite plentiful in our markets since we share our longest border with Mexico.

Mangos should be just soft to the touch, with a pronounced aroma. They can be yellow, orange, and/or red. Strawberries are grown commercially near Wichita Falls, but most Texans know Poteet as the Texas strawberry capital. Strawberries are a natural with cream, so I have paired them with generous amounts of whipped cream in this genoise-based dessert. This is a light, summery cake that should be kept under refrigeration at all times. Unlike many of the cakes in this book, which benefit from a day of resting to "marry" the flavors, this one should be assembled just before serving.

*1 recipe Genoise (see basic recipes)*

*1 pint strawberries*

*2 large mangos*

*1 1/2 pints whipping cream, chilled thoroughly in refrigerator*

*3/4 cup sugar*

*2 tablespoons Grand Marnier or Chambord liqueur*

1.  Preheat the oven to 350°F.
2.  Prepare three parchment-lined round 9-inch cake pans (see Appendix II–1).
3.  Bake the genoise in the parchment-lined cake pans until golden and firm to the touch in the center, about twenty minutes. Allow to cool.
4.  Trim and slice the strawberries, saving five of the best ones (similar in size and shape) for decorating the top. Peel, pit, and thinly slice the mangos (see Appendix II–3). Save ten uniform slices for the top of the cake.
5.  Whip the cream with the sugar to a very stiff consistency (see Appendix II–5).
6.  Place one cake layer on a plate and sprinkle with the liqueur. Spread a generous layer of whipped cream on the layer and cover it completely with the sliced strawberries. Spread a thin layer of whipped cream on the bottom of the second cake round and press down firmly on top of the first round. Sprinkle the top with liqueur and add a second layer of whipped cream. Cover this completely with mango slices. Spread the bottom of the third cake round with a thin layer of whipped cream and press down firmly on top of the second round. Sprinkle the top with liqueur.
7.  Frost the sides and top with whipped cream. Fill a pastry bag, fitted with a large star tip, with the remaining whipped cream.

**8.** Arrange the reserved mango slices pinwheel fashion in the center of the cake, overlapping them. Pipe five large rosettes of whipped cream around the edge of the cake and place a strawberry on the center of each.

**9.** Decorate the bottom edge of the cake with a shell or scroll border of whipped cream (see Appendix I).

# Babba's Apple Cake

We called my maternal grandmother "Babba." She was, without a doubt, the most incredible baker I've ever known, and she never measured anything! A pinch of this, two handfuls of that and presto . . . a perfect dough was formed right in front of your eyes. She was born in Poland and emigrated to the United States just before the Second World War. While she never quite caught on to proper English, she knew her way around a kitchen and managed to raise three wonderful daughters. Whenever she came to visit, at least two days would be spent in the kitchen baking our favorite goodies, and most requested was her apple cake. This is no ordinary cake; I don't know if you can even call it a cake. It's more like layers of puffed, sweet noodles that are filled with apples. Special thanks to my Aunt Anna (the eldest daughter) for preserving this recipe and translating it into measured quantities. The only ingredient missing from the original recipe is Babba's love, for which there is no substitute.

◇

> *4 cups all-purpose flour*
>
> *3 cups sugar*
>
> *1 teaspoon baking powder*
>
> *3 eggs*
>
> *1/2 pound unsalted butter, melted and cooled*

*3 pounds apples, Granny Smith or Macintosh*
*2 teaspoons cinnamon*

1.    Preheat the oven to 350°F.

2.    Grease a 10-by-10-by-3-inch cake pan.

3.    Melt the butter over low heat. Sift the flour with two cups of the sugar and the baking powder into a large mixing bowl. Make a well in the center. Pour the eggs into this well and mix them with a wire whip until the egg mixture is uniform. Add the cooled melted butter and stir, slowly bringing in the flour mixture to form a dough. Divide the dough into fourths and wrap in plastic.

4.    Peel, core and slice the apples (see Appendix II–3). Toss them with the remaining sugar and the cinnamon.

5.    Using a pastry cloth, roll out each piece of dough to fit the prepared pan. Don't worry about irregular shapes. Place the first layer of dough in the bottom of the pan and cover with one third of the apples. Repeat, alternating dough with apples. Cover the top with the remaining dough. Make several decorative slits in the top and sprinkle some sugar over the surface.

6.    Bake for one hour, or until juices are bubbling in the center, as well as around the edges of the cake. Cool and serve at room temperature.

# Hill Country Peach Pavé

In Austin we are especially fortunate that the Hill Country is just a short drive away and that Fredericksburg grows some of the juiciest, most flavorful peaches I've tasted. Peaches are also grown commercially in Clay, Dale, Glen Flora, Hempstead, Palestine, Rusk, and Wimberley. Most supermarkets in Texas carry local peaches from April through July, and many roadside stands also carry wonderfully tasty fruit. Unlike varieties from California and the South, Texas peaches can be picked ripe since the fruit does not have to travel far and bruising is not a problem. When selecting peaches, look for rosy fruit with a strong "peach" color and a pronounced aroma. Avoid peaches that have a greenish cast at the stem end and those that are too large (Hill Country peaches are small by nature). A pavé is a classic French cake which is rectangular or square in shape, composed of layers of genoise and filled with a buttercream.

*1 recipe Genoise (see basic recipes)*
*1/3 cup raspberry preserves*
*1 recipe Buttercream Base (see basic recipes)*

*1 teaspoon lemon juice, freshly squeezed*

*6 small peaches, ripe*

*2 fluid ounces orange curaçao*

    *toasted hazelnuts or macadamia nuts (optional)*

1.   Preheat the oven to 350°F.

2.   Prepare a parchment-lined half-sheet (12-by-16-by-1-inch) pan (see Appendix II–1).

3.   Prepare the genoise (see basic recipes).

4.   Bake the genoise in the parchment-lined sheet pan until golden and firm to the touch in the center, about twenty minutes. Allow to cool. Trim the edges and cut into four 4-by-12-inch rectangles.

5.   Prepare the buttercream base (see basic recipes).

6.   Heat the raspberry preserves and press through a fine wire mesh sieve to remove the seeds, using a spatula or the back of a spoon. Allow to cool. Add the preserves and lemon juice to the buttercream and beat in with an electric mixer.

7.   Peel, pit, and thinly slice the peaches (see Appendix II–3).

8.   Assemble the pavé in the following manner: sprinkle some curaçao on a genoise rectangle; spread a thin layer of buttercream evenly on the genoise, and add one third of the sliced peaches across the entire surface; spread a thin layer of buttercream on the bottom of a second genoise layer and press this onto the peaches.

9.   Repeat the process two more times.

10.   Ice the sides and the top of the cake with buttercream. Use a cake comb to ridge the sides of the pavé. Sprinkle toasted hazelnuts or macadamia nuts (optional) on the top. Using a pastry bag fitted with a star tip, place a shell border of buttercream along the top edges.

▼

# Apple Walnut Torte

◇

Most apple cake recipes that I've tried are rather dry in texture, set off by the moisture of the apples. I wanted a very moist cake, and to accomplish this I have adapted a recipe for a steamed apple pudding.

While New York and Washington states are major producers of apples, Texas grows some tasty varieties in Fredericksburg, Kerrville, McAllen, Medina, and Wimberley. The spices used in this recipe give a unique flavor, and the chopped walnuts add contrasting texture to this rich cake. It was called French Apple Cake until a woman from France tasted it and declared, in a way only the French can, that no one in France makes a cake like this. Oh, well . . .

*3 large apples, Granny Smith*

*1 tablespoon lemon juice, freshly squeezed*

*1/2 cup brown sugar*

*1/2 cup sugar*

*1/2 pound unsalted butter, at room temperature*

*2 eggs*

*1 tablespoon vanilla extract*

*2 cups all-purpose flour*

*2 teaspoons baking soda*

*1 teaspoon cinnamon*

*1/2 teaspoon nutmeg*

*1 cup walnuts, chopped*

*1 cup applesauce*

*2 tablespoons Grand Marnier*

*1 cup powdered sugar*

1.  Take the butter from the refrigerator at least thirty minutes before it will be needed.

2.  Preheat the oven to 350°F.

3.  Prepare a parchment-lined 10-inch springform pan (see Appendix II–1).

4.  Peel, core, and slice the apples thinly (see Appendix II–3). Add the lemon juice and toss.

5.  With the electric mixer, cream the butter with the brown and granulated sugars until fluffy, about two minutes. Add the eggs and vanilla and beat one minute. Scrape down the sides of the bowl and mix thirty seconds more.

**6.**   Mix flour, baking soda, spices, and walnuts together and, with the mixer speed on low, stir into the butter mixture. Scrape down the bowl and mix until blended. Add the applesauce and liqueur and stir to blend.

**7.**   Add half the batter to the parchment-lined springform pan and level it by smoothing with a spatula. Add the apple slices evenly across the batter. Add the remaining batter and carefully smooth it over the apples.

**8.**   Bake for forty-five minutes, or until the cake is firm to the touch in the center. Allow to cool. Remove the cake from the pan and peel off the parchment.

**9.**   Prepare a glaze by adding water, a little at a time, to the powdered sugar until the glaze is just loose enough to slowly run off a spoon. "Drizzle" the icing randomly over the cake. Allow the icing to set for thirty minutes.

# Banana Chocolate Chip Cake

◇

This cake is a true problem-solver. The problem: How did the Lord mean for us to eat bananas? At first glance it would appear that this is the perfect fruit. It's easy to carry, easy to peel, and easy to eat. The problem is that a banana achieves the stage of perfect ripeness and flavor for about three minutes. When you buy them they are hard and green, rather sour, and not flavorful at all. So you wait patiently for them to ripen (the ceremonial altar seems to be the top of the refrigerator), sampling them on a regular basis. They get better and better, but somehow not exactly right. Then, without warning, the next banana is overripe, with a pronounced alcohol and ester flavor, and the texture is shot as well. There's nothing better than a good recipe for moribund bananas. Let them try to fool you! Once they are black and mushy, they are perfect for baking, and the banana flavor becomes quite perfect in a cake. This cake is for the kid in all of us. It has bananas, of course, and chocolate chips, and a wonderfully old-fashioned chocolate frosting. What kid wouldn't like that?

*1/2 pound butter, at room temperature*

*2 cups sugar*

*1 teaspoon vanilla extract*

*1/2 teaspoon almond extract*

*3 eggs*

*6 bananas, well beyond ripe*

*3 cups all-purpose flour*

*1/2 tablespoon baking powder*

*1 teaspoon baking soda*

*2/3 cup chocolate chips*

*1 recipe Old-Fashioned Chocolate Icing (see basic recipes)*

1. Take the butter from the refrigerator at least thirty minutes before it will be needed.

2. Preheat the oven to 350°F.

3. Prepare three parchment-lined 9-inch round cake pans (see Appendix II–1).

4. With the electric mixer, cream the butter with the sugar for three minutes, until light and fluffy.

5. With the mixer running on low speed, stir in the vanilla and almond extracts. Add the eggs and mix.

6. Add the bananas and mix one minute. Scrape down the bowl and mix thirty seconds more. Do not worry if the mixture seems curdled.

7. Sift the flour with the baking powder and soda. Add this to the bowl and stir in with the mixer on low speed.

8. Fold in the chocolate chips by hand with a rubber spatula.

9. Bake in the parchment-lined cake pans for thirty minutes or until firm to the touch in the center. Allow to cool.

10. Prepare chocolate icing (see basic recipes).

11. Spread some of the chocolate icing on top of one of the cake layers and smooth with an offset spatula. Press the second layer on the first and frost with chocolate icing, using a swirling motion of the spatula.

# ‣ NUT TORTES ◄

- ‣ Native Pecan Praline Torte
- ‣ Espresso Coffee Torte
- ‣ Texas Wildflower
  Honey Spice Cake

- ‣ Grand Marnier Torte
- ‣ Pistachio White
  Chocolate Torte

# Native Pecan Praline Torte

Pecan candies, known as pralines, are very popular in Texas and Mexico and are found at the cashier's counter of most Tex-Mex restaurants. A popular dish in many local Chinese restaurants is crispy walnuts—nuts that have been boiled in syrup, then deep fried. I have combined the flavor of sweetened pecans with the technique of cooking crispy walnuts to garnish this cake with chopped, crispy pecans (which make a wonderful snack or treat on their own; I package them up as Christmas gifts in attractive tins . . . everyone loves them).

*2 cups shelled pecans*

*1 cup Crispy Pecans (see basic recipes)*

*8 eggs*

*2 tablespoons vanilla extract*

*1 cup all-purpose flour*

*1 recipe Buttercream Base (see basic recipes)*

*1 teaspoon lemon juice, freshly squeezed*

1.   Shell pecans if necessary, being careful to remove any bits of shell or membrane.

2.   Preheat the oven to 350°F.

3.   Prepare three 9-inch round parchment-lined cake pans (see Appendix II–1). Grease the sides of the pans with vegetable shortening.

4.   Grind the 2 cups of shelled pecans to a fine texture.

5.   Separate the eggs and beat the whites with one cup of sugar until firm, glossy peaks form.

6.   Beat the yolks with the remaining sugar until thick and pale in color. Add 1 tablespoon vanilla and beat thirty seconds.

7.   Mix the flour with the ground nuts and add it to the egg yolk mixture. With the mixer on low speed, stir to incorporate. Scrape down the bowl and gently mix.

8.   Fold in the egg whites until a uniform batter forms.

9.   Pour batter into the parchment-lined cake pans and bake for twenty minutes or until the center is firm to the touch. Allow to cool.

10. Prepare buttercream base (see basic recipes).

11. Beat remaining tablespoon of vanilla, one tablespoon of pecan syrup, and the lemon juice into the buttercream base. Spread buttercream between the cake layers.

12. Ice the entire cake with buttercream. When the Crispy Pecans from the basic recipe have cooled completely, chop them coarsely and press them over the surface of the cake. Refrigerate until ready to serve.

▼

# Espresso Coffee Torte

◇

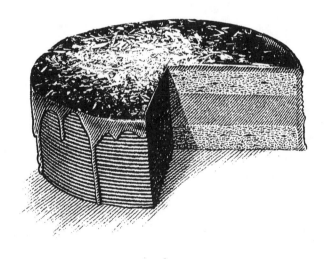

◇

This is a coffee-lover's cake. With ground espresso beans in the batter and a coffee buttercream icing (that has the taste of Häagen Dazs® coffee ice cream!), know the difference between celebes kalosie and java panjur before making this cake. Accents include the sweet tang of raspberry and the bracing bite of bitter chocolate, making this an extraordinary and unusual cake.

◇

> *1 cup walnuts*
>
> *3/4 cup all-purpose flour*
>
> *1 1/2 tablespoon espresso coffee beans, freshly ground*
>
> *6 eggs*
>
> *1 1/3 cups sugar*
>
> *1/2 teaspoon vanilla extract*
>
> *1 recipe Buttercream Base (see basic recipes)*
>
> *1 tablespoon instant espresso coffee*
>
> *1 teaspoon white rum*
>
> *1/2 cup seedless raspberry preserves*
>
> *1/2 cup Chocolate Base (see basic recipes)*

1.   Preheat the oven to 350°F.

2.   Prepare two 9-inch round parchment-lined pans (see Appendix II–1). Grease the sides of the pans with vegetable shortening.

3.   Prepare chocolate base (see basic recipes).

4.   Grind the espresso beans and walnuts fine. Toss them with the flour.

5.   Separate the eggs. Whip the whites with 2/3 cup of the sugar until firm, glossy peaks form. Do not overbeat.

6.   Beat the yolks hard with the remaining sugar until the mixture is thick and pale yellow. Add the vanilla extract. Stir in the nut/flour mixture. Scrape down the bowl and mix briefly.

7.   Fold in the egg whites to form a uniform batter. Pour batter into two 9-inch round parchment-lined pans and bake for twenty minutes or until firm to the touch in the center. Allow to cool.

8.   Remove the cakes from the pans and slice them in half laterally, forming four thin cake rounds. (Refer to the torting instructions in Appendix II–2).

9.   Prepare the buttercream base (see basic recipes).

10.   Dissolve the instant coffee into the rum to form a syrup. Beat this into the buttercream a little at a time, to taste.

11.   Spread an even layer of buttercream on the first cake round. Spread some raspberry preserves on the bottom of the second cake round and press it onto the buttercream. Spread buttercream on the second layer, raspberry preserves on the bottom of the third layer, and press together. Repeat this process with the last cake round.

12.    Ice the entire cake with buttercream and refrigerate one hour.

13.    Melt the chocolate base and pour it onto the center of the cake, spreading it across the surface with an offset spatula, allowing it to drip over the edge of the cake. Refrigerate until ready to serve.

# Texas Wildflower Honey Spice Cake

While Texas is not among the major honey-producing states, some very good honey is produced commercially in the Texas towns of Baytown, Josephine, Navasota, San Angelo, and San Antonio. (My particular favorite among producers was Niedecken Apiaries in Coupland, which produced some wonderfully exotic honeys such as cotton, mesquite, huajillo, marigold, and a wildflower variety.) I love using honey because I'm fascinated by bees: did you know that bees are not only able to perform the miracle of honey production but also mysteriously produce drone bees without fathers, having only grandfathers! This cake is an adaptation of a recipe for traditional German Christmas cookies called *lebkuchen* and is full of spices and hazelnuts as well as honey.

◇

12 *ounces cream cheese, at room temperature*

4 *ounces butter, at room temperature*

2 *tablespoons vanilla extract*

2 1/2 *cups powdered sugar*

1 *cup honey*

3/4 *cups brown sugar*

2 *tablespoons kirsch*

1/2 *cup water*

2 *eggs*

4 *teaspoons ground ginger*

1 *teaspoon cinnamon*

       *1 teaspoon allspice*

       *1 teaspoon nutmeg*

       *1 teaspoon ground cloves*

    *2 1/2 cups hazelnuts, skinned, roasted, and ground*

    *2 1/2 cups all-purpose flour*

       *1 teaspoon baking soda*

       *1 teaspoon baking powder*

1.   Take the butter and cream cheese from the refrigerator at least thirty minutes before they will be needed.

2.   Preheat the oven to 350°F.

3.   Prepare three parchment-lined 9-inch round cake pans (see Appendix II – 1).

4.   Prepare hazelnuts (see Appendix II – 4).

5.   Prepare the frosting by using the electric mixer to cream the cream cheese with the butter until fluffy. Add the vanilla. With the mixer on low speed, gradually stir in the powdered sugar and beat one minute. Refrigerate to a spreading consistency.

6.   Heat the honey to a simmer in a saucepan or microwave oven. In a large bowl dissolve the brown sugar in the honey. Stir in the kirsch and the eggs by hand using a wire whip. Add the water and stir.

7.   Mix the spices with the flour, baking powder, soda, and hazelnuts, saving about a tablespoon of nuts for garnish. Stir the mixture of dry ingredients into the liquids.

8.   Pour batter into the parchment-lined cake pans and bake for fifteen minutes, or until just firm in the center. Allow to cool.

9.   Fill and ice the cake with the frosting, using a swirling motion with the spatula to form peaks (see Appendix I). Dust the top with the reserved nuts. Using a pastry bag fitted with a large star tip, pipe a shell border of frosting along the top edge of the cake. Refrigerate until ready to serve.

# Grand Marnier Torte

This was the most popular cake at my bakery. Most people adore Grand Marnier, and rightly so. A combination of fine brandy with essence of orange, it makes a wonderful aperitif and is fabulous in desserts. This cake combines the flavors of orange, chocolate, and hazelnuts with just a hint of Grand Marnier in the cake layers.

> *8 eggs*
> *1 3/4 cups sugar*
> *1 1/2 cups hazelnuts, roasted, skinned, and ground*
> *1 cup all-purpose flour*
> *2 tablespoons vanilla extract*
> *1 recipe Buttercream Base (see basic recipes)*
> *2 tablespoons orange juice concentrate*
> *2 ounces bittersweet chocolate*
> *1 cup Chocolate Base (see basic recipes)*
> *1/2 cup orange marmalade*
> *1/4 cup Grand Marnier*

1.  Preheat the oven to 350°F.
2.  Prepare a parchment-lined half-sheet (12-by-16-by-1-inch) pan (see Appendix II–1). Grease the sides of the pan with a thin film of shortening.
3.  Prepare hazelnuts (see Appendix II–4).
4.  Prepare chocolate base (see basic recipes).
5.  Separate the eggs. Whip the whites with one cup of the sugar until firm, glossy peaks form. Do not overbeat.
6.  Mix the ground hazelnuts with the flour.
7.  Beat the yolks thoroughly with the remaining sugar until the mixture is thick and pale yellow. Add the vanilla extract. With the mixer on low speed, stir in the nut/flour mixture. Scrape down the bowl and mix briefly.

8.    Fold in the egg whites to form a uniform batter.

9.    Pour the batter into the parchment-lined half-sheet pan and bake for twenty minutes or until firm to the touch in the center. Allow to cool. Remove from the pan and peel off the parchment.

10.    Trim the cake to 8 by 16 inches by removing a 4-inch strip. Using a ruler, cut the cake into four 4-by-8-inch rectangles. Save the 4-inch strip for petit fours or another use (it makes a wonderful snack with a cup of coffee).

11.    Prepare buttercream base (see basic recipes).

12.    Beat the orange juice concentrate with the buttercream base until smooth.

13.    Sprinkle the first layer of cake with Grand Marnier. Spread a layer of buttercream on this cake rectangle. Spread a thin layer of marmalade on the bottom of the second layer and press down onto the buttercream. Repeat this process until all the layers of cake are stacked. Ice the sides and top of the cake with the remaining buttercream, making the surface as smooth as possible. Refrigerate one hour.

14.    Melt the bittersweet chocolate and the chocolate base and, with the mixer on low speed, stir them together. Beat one minute and allow to cool to spreading consistency. Spread this over the buttercream, completely covering the cake.

15.    Using a cake comb, scribe wavy ridges across the top of the cake. Using a pastry bag fitted with a small star tip, pipe a chocolate shell border along the top edges of the cake. Refrigerate until ready to serve.

# Pistachio White Chocolate Torte

After much trial and error, this became the perfect combination of flavors to accompany the subtle taste of pistachios. In addition to a white chocolate buttercream, the cake is glazed with apricot preserves, providing a tangy counterpoint to the muted flavors of the nuts and chocolate. With more than twenty buttercream flavorings and eight kinds of preserves normally at hand in the bakery, there were a possible 160 combinations to try, and we tried all of them! Most were just so-so, some were atrocious, but this combination was outstanding.

> 1 1/2 cups pistachios, shelled
> 3/4 cup all-purpose flour
> 6 eggs
> 1 1/3 cups sugar
> 1/2 teaspoon vanilla extract
> 1 teaspoon almond extract
> 6 ounces white chocolate
> 1 recipe Buttercream Base (see basic recipes)
> 1/2 cup apricot preserves

1. Preheat the oven to 350°F.
2. Shell pistachios if necessary.
3. Prepare a parchment-lined half-sheet (12-by-16-by-1-inch) pan (see Appendix II–1). Grease the sides of the pan with a thin film of shortening.
4. Grind 1 1/4 cups of pistachios fine and toss them with the flour. Reserve the remaining pistachios for garnish.
5. Separate the eggs. Whip the whites with 2/3 cup of the sugar until firm, glossy peaks form. Do not overbeat.
6. Beat the yolks thoroughly with the remaining sugar until the mixture is thick and pale yellow. Add the almond and vanilla extracts

and beat one minute. With the mixer on low speed, stir in the nut/flour mixture. Scrape down the bowl and mix briefly.

7.    Fold in the egg whites to form a uniform batter.

8.    Pour the batter into the parchment-lined half-sheet pan and bake for twenty minutes or until firm to the touch in the center. Allow to cool. Remove from the pan and peel off the parchment.

9.    Using a ruler, trim the cake to 8 by 16 inches by removing a 4-inch strip from the cake. Cut the cake into four 4-by-8-inch rectangles. Save the 4-inch strip for petit fours or another use.

10.    Prepare buttercream base (see basic recipes).

11.    Melt the white chocolate in a microwave oven at low power or in the top of a double boiler over simmering water. Beat it into the buttercream base.

12.    Puree the apricot preserves in a blender.

13.    Spread a layer of buttercream over the first cake rectangle. Spread some apricot puree on the bottom of the second cake layer and press onto the first layer. Repeat this process with all cake layers. Ice the sides and top of the cake with buttercream.

14.    Coarsely chop the remaining pistachios and press them to the sides of the cake. Using a pastry bag fitted with a small star tip, pipe buttercream shell borders along the bottom and top edges of the cake. Connect the four corner edges with an elongated, footed shell. Refrigerate until ready to serve.

# ▶ CHOCOLATE TORTES ◀

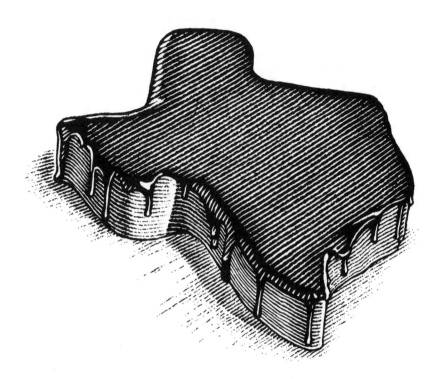

- ▶ Texas Truffle Cake
- ▶ Extra-Fat Chocolate Cake
- ▶ Belgian Chocolate Torte
- ▶ Chocolate Intemperance
- ▶ Sachertorte
- ▶ Chocolate Rum Pecan Torte
- ▶ Chocolate Giandua Torte

# Texas Truffle Cake

Chocolate truffles are so named because they are shaped like the subterranean fungus that grows at the base of certain oak trees in Italy and France. Used in the preparation of fine, savory dishes, French truffles are found primarily in Périgord (these are considered the finest of all) as well as in Normandy and Burgundy. About ten years ago it was noted that the Texas Hill Country, Dripping Springs in particular, had a microclimate and soil conditions very similar to those of Périgord and supported the growth of fine oak trees. Several enterprising businessmen inoculated the Texas oaks in the hope of producing Texas truffles. We'll have to wait and see; it takes at least ten years to establish the fungal colonies. In the meantime I give you the Texas truffle cake, a rich chocolate treat filled with a chocolate truffle mixture and shaped like the state of Texas (a much more pleasant shape than that of a subterranean fungus).

> *1 recipe Basic Chocolate Cake (see basic recipes)*
> *3 cups Chocolate Base (see basic recipes)*
> *8 ounces bittersweet chocolate, chopped into small pieces*
> *1/2 cup raspberry preserves*
> *1 recipe Old-Fashioned Chocolate Frosting (see basic recipes)*

1.   Preheat the oven to 350°F.
2.   Prepare two parchment-lined half-sheet (12-by-16-by-1-inch) pans (see Appendix II–1).
3.   Prepare chocolate base (see basic recipes).
4.   Prepare the basic chocolate cake recipe.
5.   Bake the chocolate cake in the parchment-lined half-sheet pans for twenty minutes or until just firm to the touch in the center. Allow to cool. Cut each rectangle in half across the 16-inch side and stack the four pieces. Refrigerate for three to four hours.
6.   Prepare a parchment template of the shape of Texas, about 9 inches at its widest dimension, to approximate the size of the stacked cake.

Place the Texas template on the stacked cake layers and cut out the shape of Texas. Save the trimmings for another use.

7. Heat two cups chocolate base in a microwave set on low or over simmering water in the top of a double boiler until warm and pourable.

8. Melt the chocolate in a microwave set on low or in the top of a double boiler.

9. Mix the melted chocolate with the chocolate base until smooth (this is the truffle mixture) and divide this mixture into three equal portions. Spread one-third of this filling on each layer as you assemble the three bottom layers.

10. Microwave the raspberry preserves on medium or warm in double boiler. Press through a fine sieve using the back of a spoon to remove the seeds. Glaze the sides and top of the cake with the preserves and chill thirty minutes.

11. Prepare chocolate frosting (see basic recipes).

12. Frost the entire cake with the chocolate frosting, carefully smoothing the top and sides. Refrigerate thirty minutes.

13. Microwave the remaining cup of chocolate base on medium or warm in a double boiler until pourable but not hot. Remove the cake from the refrigerator and carefully pour the chocolate over the top of the cake, starting in the center. As it spreads, use an offset spatula to cover the entire top of the cake and allow small amounts to drip neatly down the sides of the cake. Refrigerate immediately to set the glaze (which will remain shiny).

14. If you so desire, form a small rose with any remaining chocolate frosting, using a pastry bag and rose tip. Place this rose on your favorite city or town. Add a chocolate leaf for additional accent. Refrigerate until ready to serve.

# Extra-Fat Chocolate Cake

◇

According to pop culture "less is more." When it comes to chocolate, nothing could be further from the truth. To this end I have developed an old-fashioned chocolate cake that will satisfy the most demanding chocoholic. This recipe is the product of much experimentation.

While there are hundreds of cookbooks with chocolate cake recipes, none had the combination of moistness, dark color, and density that I was seeking. After developing the prototype to this cake, I invoked the spirit of "more is better" and doubled the amount of chocolate added to the batter, hence the name. This cake reminds me of the fifties, when moms wore aprons and dads wore hats. When I make this cake, I almost expect Wally and the Beaver to come in the kitchen door and ask for "a hunk o' cake and some milk."

2 tablespoons cocoa powder

2 1/3 cups all-purpose flour

2 teaspoons baking powder

2 teaspoons baking soda

8 ounces bittersweet chocolate

2 cups hot water, about 120°F

6 ounces unsalted butter, at room temperature

1 2/3 cups sugar

1 recipe Old-Fashioned Chocolate Frosting (see basic recipes)

1.    Take the butter from the refrigerator at least thirty minutes before it will be needed.

2.    Preheat the oven to 350°F.

3.    Prepare two parchment-lined 9-inch round cake pans (see Appendix II–1).

4.    Sift the cocoa, flour, baking powder, and baking soda together.

5.    Shave some chocolate from the block and reserve it for the top garnish. Chop the remainder very fine and add it to the hot water in a bowl. Let the mixture stand for five minutes, then whisk by hand to blend.

6.    Using the electric mixer, cream the butter with the sugar for two minutes, until pale and fluffy.

7.    Carefully add half the dry ingredients to the butter mixture and stir in with the mixer on low speed.

8.    Add half the chocolate mixture and stir. Scrape down the sides of the bowl and stir thirty seconds.

9. Repeat with the remaining dry ingredients and chocolate mixture. Stir to form a smooth batter.

10. Bake in parchment-lined cake pans for twenty minutes or until firm to the touch at the center. Do not be concerned if the cakes are cracked and ugly. (We used to call them "gorilla cakes" at the bakery!)

11. Allow the cakes to cool thoroughly and refrigerate them until firm. Remove them from the pans and trim the sides and tops with a serrated knife.

12. Prepare chocolate frosting (see basic recipes).

13. Fill and ice the cake with the chocolate frosting, using swirling motions with the spatula. Shave some chocolate over the top. Decorate the bottom with a shell border, using a pastry bag fitted with a star tip. Refrigerate until ready to serve.

▼

# Belgian Chocolate Torte

◇

Quality chocolate is produced in several European countries, notably Switzerland, France, and Belgium. While good chocolate is produced in the United States, it just cannot compare to the imports. The Swiss are noted for producing the finest chocolates, but I prefer the Belgian varieties and besides, can you really trust people who mow the sides of their mountains? Once you've chosen a country, a type of chocolate must be selected as well. I prefer a bittersweet type, one that has a bite to it and almost burns the back of the throat. Do not rely on the manufacturer's description, as some Swiss semisweet chocolates are, in fact, bittersweet. This cake is very, very dense and should be baked in a slow oven to produce its unique texture, a cross between cake and fudge. Serve with a raspberry puree and a dollop of unsweetened whipped cream for a special treat.

*6 eggs*

*1 3/4 cups sugar*

*1/2 pound unsalted butter*

*3/4 cup milk*

*1 1/2 pounds bittersweet chocolate, chopped very fine*

*2/3 cup heavy cream*

*1 1/2 cups all-purpose flour*

*1/4 cup cocoa*

*2 teaspoons baking powder*

*Powdered sugar (optional)*

*Chocolate Ganache (optional; see basic recipes)*

*Raspberry puree (optional)*

*Whipped cream (optional; see Appendix II – 5)*

1.   Preheat the oven to 300°F.

2.   Prepare a parchment-lined 10-inch springform pan (see Appendix II – 1).

3.   Prepare ganache if desired (see basic recipes).

4.   Separate the eggs. Using the electric mixer, whip the whites with 3/4 cup of the sugar to form firm peaks. Do not overbeat them. Set aside.

5.   Using the mixer, cream the butter with the remaining sugar. While this is mixing, scald the milk, then pour it over the chocolate to melt it. If the chocolate does not fully melt, carefully microwave the mixture on low or in the top of a double boiler over simmering water. With the mixer on low speed, stir the chocolate mixture until it is smooth.

6.   Add the egg yolks to the butter mixture. Beat until smooth. Scrape down the sides of the bowl and beat thirty seconds more.

7.   Add the chocolate mixture and stir until smooth. Scrape down the sides of the bowl and add the cream. Beat for one minute.

8.   Sift the flour, cocoa, and baking powder together and add to the batter, stirring carefully. Scrape down the bowl and mix thirty seconds.

9.   Gently fold in the egg whites until the batter is uniform in texture.

10.   Add the batter to the parchment-lined springform pan and bake for one hour and twenty minutes or until just firm to the touch in the center.

11.   Allow the cake to cool. Refrigerate several hours. Remove the cake from the pan and peel off the parchment. The top may be dusted with cocoa powder or powdered sugar, or left plain. To "gild the lily,"

spread some chocolate ganache over the top and form ridges with a cake comb. Refrigerate until ready to serve.

# Chocolate Intemperance

◇

The ultimate chocolate dessert deserves a special name. This name has been around for at least twenty years, but what follows is a totally original recipe, and I think it is a definite improvement over all other versions. Typically, this dessert would be described as a chocolate mousse filling, surrounded by a brownie "crust," topped with a chocolate ganache. My version's filling goes far beyond a mousse (which means "foam" in French), as it has an especially dense yet velvety texture. Other attempts to create names connoting the ultimate in chocolate indulgence have included "chocolate orgasm" (am I the only one who thinks this a disgusting name for a dessert?) and "death by chocolate" (hardly appealing either). I believe that when you hear a great name, steal it! According to Webster, *intemperance* is a noun meaning lack of self-restraint, overindulgence.

Perfect!

1/2 recipe Basic Chocolate Cake (see basic recipes)

2 pounds bittersweet chocolate, chopped very fine

1 1/2 cups heavy cream

1/3 cup sugar

2 tablespoons unflavored gelatin

1/4 cup water

1 cup milk

5 egg yolks

1 1/2 cups Chocolate Base (see basic recipes)

1 recipe Chocolate Ganache (see basic recipes)

1 teaspoon orange juice concentrate

1.    Preheat the oven to 350°F.

2.    Prepare a parchment-lined half-sheet (12-by-16-by-1-inch) pan (see Appendix II – 1).

3.    Prepare the chocolate base (see basic recipes).

4.    Prepare the basic chocolate cake (see basic recipes).

5.    Bake the chocolate cake in the parchment-lined half-sheet pan for fifteen minutes or until firm to the touch in the center. Allow to cool. Freeze thoroughly.

6.    Remove the cake from the freezer, invert it on a counter and peel off the parchment. Take a 10-inch springform pan (no preparation necessary) and line it with chocolate cake as follows. Lay the bottom of the springform pan near one corner of the cake and cut out a circle of cake. Using a ruler, cut 2-inch strips of cake. Place the circle in the bottom of the pan and line the sides with the strips of cake. Do this quickly or the strips will become soft and tend to crumble. If the cake softens, return the cut pieces to the freezer until firm. When the interior of the springform pan is completely lined with cake, return it to the freezer.

7.    Place the chopped chocolate in a microwave oven on medium or in the top of a double boiler over simmering water and carefully melt it. Be sure that the chocolate is completely melted and is no warmer than about 100°F.

8.    Whip the cream with the sugar until quite stiff (see Appendix II – 5). Chill until needed.

9.    Place the gelatin in the bottom of a large mixing bowl and add the water to it. Allow to stand about five minutes.

10.    Scald the milk. Add it to the gelatin and, with the mixer on low speed, stir to dissolve. Add the egg yolks and stir to mix.

11.    While stirring, gradually add the melted chocolate. Mix two minutes.

12.    Warm the chocolate base as you did the chopped chocolate in step 7 and add it to the mixture. Scrape down the sides of the bowl and mix one minute.

13.    Fold in the whipped cream and stir gently until uniform.

14.    Remove the pan from the freezer and pour in the chocolate filling. Refrigerate overnight.

15.    Prepare chocolate ganache (see basic recipes).

16.    Carefully remove the dessert from the pan. Add the orange juice concentrate to the ganache and top dessert with this mixture. Refrigerate until ready to serve.

# Sachertorte

Controversy should surround politics, not pastry. Yet the sachertorte is probably the most controversial of all cakes. A seven-year lawsuit finally settled the claim to the "original" sachertorte in Vienna. In a move that would make any politician proud, the courts agreed to allow two different cakes made by two different entities to be sold as sacher-torte in Vienna! One is a standard size cake and the other is quite small. One has three layers, the other has only one. At least they are both chocolate, glazed with apricot preserves, and covered with a chocolate icing. It is believed that this cake was created by Franz Sacher, pastry chef to Prince Metternich, and descendants of Herr Sacher lay claim to one of the authentic cakes. The Hotel Sacher is the other legally approved producer of sachertorte. Adding to the confusion are the scores of recipes published in cookbooks, no two alike! This version is an Americanized one in that the dry breadcrumbs used in many of the European recipes have been omitted to improve moistness and change the texture somewhat.

*6 eggs*

*1 3/4 cups sugar*

*8 ounces unsalted butter*

*3/4 cup milk*

*16 ounces bittersweet chocolate, chopped very fine*

*2/3 cup heavy cream*

*1 cup all-purpose flour*

*1/2 cup cocoa*

*2 teaspoons baking powder*

*1 cup apricot preserves*

*1 cup Chocolate Base (see basic recipes)*

1.  Preheat the oven to 350°F.
2.  Prepare three 9-inch round parchment-lined cake pans (see Appendix II–1).

3.   Prepare chocolate base (see basic recipes).

4.   Separate the eggs. Using the electric mixer, whip the whites with 3/4 cup of the sugar to form firm, glossy peaks. Do not overbeat. Set them aside.

5.   Using the electric mixer, cream the butter with the remaining sugar. While this is mixing, scald the milk, then pour it over 14 ounces of the chocolate to melt it. If some of the chocolate remains unmelted, carefully microwave this mixture on low or heat in a double boiler over simmering water. With the mixer on low speed, stir the chocolate mixture until smooth.

6.   Add the egg yolks to the butter mixture. Beat until smooth. Scrape down the sides of the bowl and beat thirty seconds more.

7.   Add the chocolate mixture and stir until smooth. Scrape down the sides of the bowl and add the cream. Beat for one minute.

8.   Sift the flour, cocoa, and baking powder together and add them to the batter, stirring carefully. Scrape down the bowl and mix thirty seconds.

9.   Gently fold in the egg whites until the batter is uniform in texture.

10.   Bake in parchment-lined cake pans for thirty minutes or until firm to the touch in the center. Allow to cool. Refrigerate several hours.

11.   Remove the cakes from the pans and trim edges with a serrated knife.

12.   Puree the apricot preserves in a blender until smooth. Spread generous amounts of the apricot between each layer, pressing down firmly as you add new layers. Glaze the sides and the top of the cake. Refrigerate at least one hour before frosting the cake.

13.   Melt the remaining two ounces of chocolate in a microwave oven or double boiler. Stir it into the chocolate base until smooth. Ice the cake with this frosting. With a pastry bag fitted with a plain tip, write the name "Sacher" in script across the top of the cake with icing. Refrigerate until ready to serve.

# Chocolate Rum Pecan Torte

This torte is a flourless cake that uses ground nuts as a substitute. Many people are surprised when they hear of a cake being flourless and speak almost reverentially about the cake they have just tried. Unlike breads, which rely on a complex, three-dimensional glutenin network derived from wheat proteins to provide structure, cakes are dependent on the egg proteins and wheat starches for structure. For delicate cakes, a special cake flour can be used, derived from soft wheats that are especially low in protein content. Notice in this and other flourless cake recipes the inordinately large number of eggs called for. The eggs tend to compensate for the loss of available starch when nuts are used as the "base."

*1 1/2 pounds bittersweet chocolate, chopped very fine*
*8 eggs*
*1 1/2 cups sugar*
*10 ounces butter, unsalted and at room temperature*
*3 fluid ounces dark rum*
*1 pound shelled pecans*

1. Take the butter from the refrigerator at least thirty minutes before it will be needed.
2. Shell the pecans if necessary, being careful to remove any bits of shell or membrane, and reserve 8 of the best for garnish.
3. Preheat the oven to 325°F.
4. Prepare a parchment-lined 10-inch springform pan (see Appendix II–1).
5. Melt one pound of the chocolate in a microwave oven at half power, or over simmering water in the top of a double boiler.
6. In an electric mixer, separate the eggs and whip the whites with 3/4 cup of the sugar until firm peaks form and the egg whites are glossy.
7. Using the mixer, cream eight ounces of the butter and remaining sugar together until light and fluffy, about two minutes.

8.   Heat the rum to a simmer to evaporate the alcohol and allow to cool.

9.   Add the melted chocolate to the butter mixture and beat two minutes. Scrape down the sides of the bowl and mix thirty seconds more.

10.   Add the rum.

11.   Add the egg yolks, scrape down the bowl, and beat one minute.

12.   Grind the pecans to a fine meal and stir them into the batter.

13.   Gently fold in the egg whites and stir to a uniform consistency.

14.   Pour batter into the parchment-lined springform pan and bake for one hour or until set in the middle.

15.   Allow to cool and refrigerate several hours. Remove the cake from the pan and peel off the parchment.

16.   Prepare the glaze by melting 8 ounces of chocolate with 2 ounces of butter. Place the cake on a wire rack and carefully pour the glaze over the cake, using a spatula on the sides to ensure complete covering. Allow the glaze to set.

17.   Garnish with reserved pecan halves.

# Chocolate Giandua Torte

Giandua, also spelled g-i-a-n-d-u-j-a, is a type of "chocolate" made with ultrafine ground hazelnuts, cocoa butter, and sugar. Its taste is exquisite. We will use the giandua in copious amounts to flavor a buttercream that will frost a rich chocolate cake filled with ganache mixed with chopped hazelnuts, often referred to as Président's ganache.

*1 recipe Basic Chocolate Cake (see basic recipes)*

*1 cup hazelnuts, skinned*

*1 recipe Ganache (see basic recipes)*

*8 ounces giandua (more for garnish)*

*1 recipe Buttercream Base (see basic recipes)*

*2 fluid ounces Frangelico or hazelnut liqueur*
*1 ounce dark chocolate*

1.  Preheat the oven to 350°F.
2.  Prepare three parchment-lined 9-inch round cake pans (see Appendix II–1).
3.  Skin hazelnuts according to instructions in Appendix II–4.
4.  Prepare basic chocolate cake (see basic recipes).
5.  Prepare ganache (see basic recipes).
6.  Bake the chocolate cake in parchment-lined pans twenty minutes or until firm to the touch in the center. Allow to cool and refrigerate several hours.
7.  Prepare buttercream (see basic recipes).
8.  Save five of the most uniform hazelnuts for garnish and chop the rest fine. Reserve 1/4 cup of the chopped nuts for garnish.
9.  Fold the remaining chopped nuts into the ganache.
10.  Melt the giandua in a microwave oven at low power or in the top of a double boiler over simmering water, and stir it into the buttercream base with the mixer on low speed. Beat one minute until smooth and glossy.
11.  Remove the cakes from the pans and cut each in half laterally so that you have six thin cake circles (this is referred to as "torting" the layers; see Appendix II–2).
12.  Sprinkle some Frangelico on the first layer, then spread a generous amount of ganache evenly across the layer. Place a second cake circle on this and sprinkle with Frangelico. Spread an even amount of buttercream on the second layer of cake (equal in thickness to the ganache). Press the third cake circle on top, sprinkle liqueur, and add another layer of ganache. Repeat with buttercream and then ganache. At this point there should be three ganache layers alternating with two buttercream layers. Refrigerate one hour.
13.  Remove the cake from the refrigerator and trim the sides using a serrated knife. Ice the sides and top of the cake with buttercream, making the top as smooth as possible.
14.  Press the reserved chopped hazelnuts around the side of the cake.
15.  Using a pastry bag fitted with a large star tip, pipe five large rosettes of buttercream evenly spaced near the edge of the cake. Apply a bottom shell border of buttercream.

16.    Place a whole hazelnut in the center of each rosette.

17.    For a final touch, separately melt a little dark chocolate and some giandua and drizzle some of each across the top of the cake. Refrigerate until ready to serve.

# ▸ C A S S A T E ◂

SICILY

PALERMO

MESSINA

CATANIA

AGRIGENTO

*MEDITERRANEAN SEA*

- ▸ Cassata Bella
- ▸ Cappuccino Cassata
- ▸ Chocolate Cassata
- ▸ Neapolitan Cassata

# Cassate

A cassata is a Sicilian specialty cake made of rich butter sponge cake filled with a sweetened ricotta cream. While the Italians do not normally indulge in rich desserts at the end of a meal, they do frequent pastry shops for espresso and a rich dessert in the evenings. The butter sponge is called *genoese*, which in French becomes *genoise*. Many Gallic specialties originated in Italy, having been transported by the Medicis through marriage with members of the French royal court. What follows are four variations on the theme: Cassata Bella—a classic vanilla-flavored cassata; Cappuccino Cassata—with a mocha filling; Chocolate Cassata—an all-chocolate excursion (this is so incredibly chocolatey it should be near the top of the list of chocolate tortes); and Neapolitan Cassata—alternating layers of vanilla, chocolate, and raspberry ricotta fillings.

A word on ricotta cheeses: although I usually do not endorse specific brands, I have had great difficulty with most supermarket ricottas. Frigo® brand is without a doubt the best and does not usually need draining. I highly recommend it for all ricotta fillings.

# Cassata Bella

*1 recipe Genoise (see basic recipes)*
*1 pound Frigo® whole milk ricotta*
*1 cup whipping cream*
*1/2 cup sugar*
*1 teaspoon vanilla extract*
*2 fluid ounces orange curaçao*
*4 ounces bittersweet chocolate*
*1/2 recipe Buttercream Base (see basic recipes)*

*1 cup Chocolate Base (see basic recipes)*
*Chocolate vermicelli*
*Chopped hazelnuts*

1. If the ricotta contains excess liquid, drain it in a cheesecloth-lined strainer for two hours.
2. Preheat the oven to 350°F.
3. Prepare a half-sheet (12-by-16-by-1-inch) parchment-lined pan (see Appendix II – 1).
4. Prepare chocolate base (see basic recipes).
5. Prepare genoise (see basic recipes).
6. Bake the genoise in a parchment-lined half-sheet pan for fifteen minutes or until firm to the touch at the center. Allow to cool. Remove from the pan and peel off the parchment. Using a ruler, cut this cake into four 4-by-12-inch pieces.
7. Whip the cream with 1/4 cup of the sugar to form stiff peaks (see Appendix II – 5). Refrigerate until needed.
8. Beat the ricotta with the remaining sugar, the vanilla, and one teaspoon of the orange curaçao until the sugar dissolves, about one minute. Gently fold in the whipped cream.
9. Sprinkle the first genoise layer with curaçao and spread a generous layer of ricotta filling over it. Add the second layer and repeat with the curaçao and ricotta filling. Continue this process for the remaining layers. Using a spatula, press ricotta filling into the sides of the cake to fill in any gaps in the layers.
10. Place the cassata in the freezer for several hours. Remove and trim the sides with a serrated knife.
11. Prepare buttercream base (see basic recipes).
12. Melt the bittersweet chocolate, add half of it to the buttercream, and beat until smooth and shiny. Melt the chocolate base and beat in the remaining bittersweet chocolate.
13. Top the cassata with a layer of buttercream equal in thickness to the ricotta layers. Refrigerate until firm.
14. Frost the entire cake with the chocolate icing, using swirling motions to form peaks. Sprinkle the top with chocolate vermicelli (sprinkles or "jimmies") and chopped hazelnuts. Refrigerate until ready to serve.

# Cappuccino Cassata

*1 recipe Genoise (see basic recipes)*

*1 pound Frigo® whole milk ricotta*

*1 cup whipping cream*

*1/2 cup sugar*

*1 teaspoon vanilla extract*

*2 fluid ounces orange curaçao*

*1 tablespoon instant coffee*

*1 teaspoon white rum*

*1 1/2 cups Chocolate Base (see basic recipes)*

*1/2 recipe Buttercream Base (see basic recipes)*

*4 ounces bittersweet chocolate (plus a small
amount for top garnish)*

1. If the ricotta contains excess liquid, drain it in a cheesecloth-lined strainer for two hours.

2. Preheat the oven to 350°F and prepare a half-sheet (12-by-16-by-1-inch) parchment-lined pan (see Appendix II–1).

3. Prepare chocolate base (see basic recipes).

4. Prepare genoise (see basic recipes).

5. Bake genoise in the parchment-lined pan for fifteen minutes or until firm to the touch at the center. Allow to cool. Remove from the pan and peel off the parchment. Using a ruler, cut this cake into four 4-by-12-inch pieces.

6. Whip the cream with 1/4 cup of the sugar to form stiff peaks (see Appendix II–5). Refrigerate until needed.

7. Beat the ricotta with the remaining sugar, the vanilla, and one teaspoon of the orange curaçao until the sugar dissolves, about one minute. Gently fold in the whipped cream.

8. Dissolve the instant coffee in the rum to form a syrup. Melt 1/2 cup of the chocolate base and add half of the coffee mixture to it. With the mixer on low speed, stir to incorporate completely.

9.  Gently fold 1/4 cup of this mocha chocolate into the ricotta filling and mix until smooth.

10. Sprinkle the first genoise layer with liqueur and spread a generous layer of ricotta filling over it. Spread a thin layer of mocha chocolate on the bottom of the second layer and press down onto the first. Continue this process for the remaining layers. Using a spatula, press ricotta filling into the sides of the cake to fill in any gaps in the layers.

11. Place the cassata in the freezer for several hours. Remove and trim the sides with a serrated knife.

12. Prepare buttercream base (see basic recipes).

13. Melt the bittersweet chocolate, add half of it to the buttercream, and beat until smooth and shiny. With the mixer on low speed, stir the remaining coffee/rum mixture into the buttercream. Melt the chocolate base and beat in the remaining bittersweet chocolate.

14. Ice the entire cassata with buttercream. Refrigerate until firm.

15. Frost the entire cake with the chocolate icing, making the surface as smooth as possible. Using a pastry bag fitted with a star tip, pipe a shell border along the top edges with the chocolate icing. I like to start the shell tops in alternating and opposite directions in order to give the border a woven look. With a plain tip, add dots of buttercream between the shells. Shave chocolate across the top of the cake. Refrigerate until ready to serve.

# Chocolate Cassata

*1 recipe Chocolate Genoise (see basic recipes)*
*1 pound Frigo® whole milk ricotta*
*1 cup whipping cream*
*1/2 cup sugar*
*1 teaspoon vanilla extract*
*2 fluid ounces orange curaçao*
*4 ounces bittersweet chocolate*
*1/2 cup Chocolate Base (see basic recipes)*
*1/2 recipe Buttercream Base (see basic recipes)*
*1 recipe Chocolate Frosting (see basic recipes)*
*giandua (hazelnut chocolate) for garnish*
*white chocolate (for garnish)*

1.   If the ricotta contains excess liquid, drain it in a cheesecloth-lined strainer for two hours.

2.   Preheat the oven to 350°F.

3.   Prepare three 9-inch parchment-lined round cake pans (Appendix II–1).

4.   Prepare chocolate base (see basic recipes).

5.   Prepare chocolate genoise (see basic recipes).

6.   Bake the genoise in the parchment-lined pans for twenty minutes or until firm to the touch in the center. Allow to cool. Slice each round laterally to form two thin cake circles, six in all (see Appendix II–2 on torting layers).

7.   Using the electric mixer, whip the cream with 1/4 cup of the sugar to form stiff peaks (see Appendix II–5). Refrigerate until needed.

8.   Beat the ricotta with the remaining sugar, the vanilla, and one teaspoon of the orange curaçao until the sugar dissolves, about one minute. Gently fold in the whipped cream.

9.   In a microwave oven or double boiler, melt the chocolate base and, when it is cool to the touch, add it to the ricotta filling. Stir by hand to blend.

10.   Sprinkle the first cake layer with orange curaçao. Spread a layer of chocolate ricotta filling on the cake. Add the second cake layer and repeat with curaçao and ricotta filling. Continue with remaining cake layers and top with the last layer. Spread ricotta filling into the sides of the cake to fill in any gaps in the layers. Freeze for several hours. Trim the sides of the cassata with a serrated knife to smooth the edges.

11.   Prepare buttercream base (see basic recipes).

12.   In a microwave oven on low or in the top of a double boiler over simmering water, carefully melt the bittersweet chocolate. With the mixer on low speed, stir into buttercream.

13.   Frost the entire cake with the chocolate buttercream and refrigerate one hour.

14.   Ice the cake with the chocolate frosting, making the surface as smooth as possible. Using a pastry bag fitted with a small star tip, pipe a shell border along the bottom edge and five rosettes along the top edge. Drizzle some melted giandua and white chocolate over the top. Refrigerate until ready to serve.

# Neapolitan Cassata

◇

*1 recipe Genoise (see basic recipes)*

*1 pound Frigo® whole milk ricotta*

*1 cup whipping cream*

*1/2 cup sugar*

*4 teaspoons vanilla extract*

*2 fluid ounces orange curaçao*

*2 tablespoons seedless raspberry preserves*

*1 cup Chocolate Base (see basic recipes)*

*1 tablespoon lemon juice, freshly squeezed*

*1/2 recipe Buttercream Base (see basic recipes)*

1.   If the ricotta contains excess liquid, drain it in a cheesecloth-lined strainer for two hours.

2.   Preheat the oven to 350°F.

3.   Prepare three parchment-lined 9-inch round cake pans (see Appendix II–1).

4.   Prepare chocolate base (see basic recipes).

5.   Prepare genoise (see basic recipes).

6.   Bake the genoise in the parchment-lined pans for twenty minutes or until firm to the touch in the center. Allow to cool. Remove the cakes from the pans and cut each round laterally with a serrated knife to form six thin cake rounds (see Appendix II–2).

7.   Whip the cream with 1/4 cup of the sugar to form stiff peaks (see Appendix II–5). Refrigerate until needed.

8.   Beat the ricotta with the remaining sugar, 1 teaspoon vanilla, and one teaspoon of the orange curaçao until the sugar dissolves, about one minute. Gently fold in the whipped cream.

9.   Divide the ricotta into five equal portions, reserving two portions which will be the vanilla filling. With the mixer on low speed, combine two portions of the ricotta and add the raspberry preserves, stirring gently to blend. Melt one tablespoon of chocolate base and stir it into the remaining portion of ricotta.

10.   Sprinkle the first cake layer with curaçao and spread half of the raspberry filling on this layer. Top with a cake circle, sprinkle with curaçao and spread half of the vanilla filling on it. Add the third cake circle, sprinkle with curaçao, and spread the chocolate ricotta filling on it. Sprinkle some curaçao on the fourth cake layer and add the remaining vanilla filling. Place the fifth cake circle, sprinkle the curaçao, and spread the remaining raspberry layer. Top with the last cake circle. Place the cassata in the freezer for several hours. Trim the sides of the cake with a serrated knife.

11.   Prepare buttercream base (see basic recipes).

12.   Beat the lemon juice and one tablespoon of vanilla extract into the buttercream base. Spread this evenly over the entire cake, smoothing the surface as you go. With a cake comb, ridge the sides of the cake. Refrigerate one hour.

13.   Melt the remaining chocolate base and pour it over the top of the cake, starting in the center. Use an offset spatula to help spread the chocolate evenly and allow small amounts to drip over the edge. Refrigerate until ready to serve.

# ▸TARTS AND PIES◂

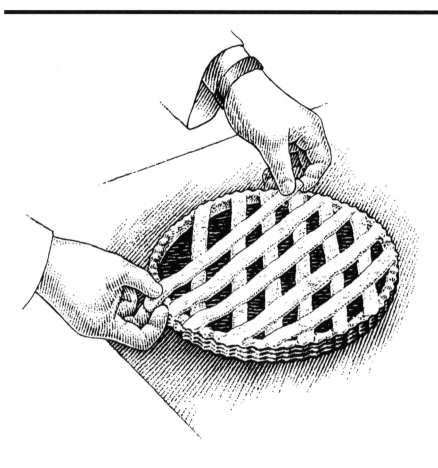

- ▸ Clarksville Lemon Almond Tart

- ▸ Linzertorte

- ▸ Crostata di Nocino

- ▸ Appeltaart

- ▸ Jalapeño Pecan Pie

- ▸ Bourbon Macadamia Pie

- ▸ Fudge Pecan Pie

- ▸ Apple Chèvre Pie

- ▸ Double Fudge Chocolate Cream Pie

# Clarksville Lemon Almond Tart

Clarksville is a historical Austin neighborhood that provided housing for ex-slaves in the mid-to-late 1800s. Recent gentrification of the area has created an interesting mix of races and cultures: blacks and whites, professors and laborers, aging hippies and executives, retired people and college students throng to Clarksville's restaurants, grocery stores, and cleaners, not to mention an old-fashioned pharmacy with a lunch counter. Clarksville Cafe was one of Austin's most popular restaurants in the eighties, and this was one of their most popular desserts.

*1/2 recipe Tart Dough (see basic recipes)*
*1 cup lemon juice, freshly squeezed*
*1/4 cup water*
*1 cup sugar*
*1 teaspoon unflavored gelatin*
*3 tablespoons cornstarch*
*1 teaspoon lemon zest*
*3 egg yolks*
*8 ounces almond paste or marzipan*
*1/2 cup sliced almonds*

1. Preheat the oven to 350°F.
2. Prepare tart dough (see basic recipes).
3. Using a pastry cloth, roll out the tart dough into a circle of approximately 12 inches. Press the tart dough into an ungreased 10-inch tart pan with a removable bottom. Press a 9-inch round cake pan into the center to help keep the shape of the tart. Bake for twenty minutes or just until it turns golden around the edges. Remove the cake pan from the center and bake five minutes more. Allow to cool.
4. Put the lemon juice and half of the water into a stainless steel or other nonreactive saucepan. Add the sugar and heat the mixture. In a small cup add one tablespoon of water to the gelatin and allow to stand. With a wire whip, stir the remaining water into the cornstarch

to form a slurry (a thin paste). Add this to the lemon juice mixture and stir to dissolve. Bring this mixture to a boil. When thick, add the softened gelatin and stir to dissolve. Add the lemon zest.

5. Remove the pan from the heat and beat some of the hot filling into the egg yolks to temper them. Add the yolks to the lemon filling and cook over low heat until the mixture just begins to simmer.

6. Remove the filling from the heat, place a piece of plastic film over the surface, and allow the filling to cool.

7. Roll out the almond paste between sheets of plastic wrap in a 10-inch circle to fit in the bottom of the tart crust. Press it into the bottom and add the lemon filling. Cover with plastic and refrigerate until set.

8. Toast the almonds in a heavy skillet until just browned. Crush them slightly and sprinkle them across the surface of the tart. Refrigerate until ready to serve.

# Linzertorte

The linzertorte is a classic Viennese pastry. It can be made with ground almonds or hazelnuts. Although I try to use hazelnuts whenever possible, I think that the almonds make a superior tart, allowing the raspberry filling to stand out and complement the nutty flavor. While the name *linzertorte* evokes romantic images of Old Vienna, in fact it is named for the city of Linz, one of the most industrialized and over-modernized cities in all of Europe.

*1/2 pound unsalted butter, at room temperature*

*1 cup sugar*

*4 egg yolks*

*1 1/2 cups all-purpose flour*

*1 1/2 cups ground almonds*

*1/2 teaspoon ground cinnamon*

*1/4 teaspoon ground cloves*

*1 cup seedless raspberry preserves*
*sugar or apricot preserves for top of tart*

1.    Take the butter from the refrigerator at least thirty minutes before it will be needed.
2.    Preheat the oven to 350°F.
3.    With the electric mixer, cream the butter with the sugar until fluffy, about four minutes.
4.    Add the egg yolks and beat them in. Scrape down the bowl and beat two minutes.
5.    Mix the flour, ground almonds, and spices together and add to the butter mixture. With the mixer on low speed, stir to form a dough. Scrape down the sides and mix briefly.
6.    Wrap in plastic and refrigerate several hours.
7.    Cut off approximately one fourth of the dough and flatten it with your palm. Return it to the refrigerator; this will form the lattice top. With the aid of a pastry cloth, quickly roll out the larger portion of dough and press it into a 10-inch tart pan with a removable bottom so as to line the bottom of the pan with dough. Place it in the refrigerator to firm up.
8.    Heat the raspberry preserves until thin but not hot. Remove the pan from the refrigerator and pour the raspberry preserves into it, turning the pan to coat the dough evenly. Roll out the reserved dough and cut it into 3/4-inch strips, forming a lattice across the top. Do not attempt to weave the strips.
9.    Either sprinkle the top lattice with sugar now or glaze the cooled tart after baking with some heated apricot preserves.
10.    Bake for thirty minutes or until the top is browned. Allow to cool.

# Crostata di Nocino

◇

A crostata is an Italian pie. This one has a double crust with a walnut filling that is like candy. It's incredibly dense and sweet, and a little goes a long way. The Swiss make a nusstorte which is almost identical to this. The filling, when cooled, can be made into balls which can be dipped in tempered chocolate or rolled in chopped nuts to make little "treats."

◇

*3 cups heavy cream*

*1 1/2 cups sugar*

*1/2 cup light corn syrup*

*1 tablespoon kirsch*

*1 tablespoon orange curaçao*

*1 pound walnuts, chopped fine (not ground)*

*1 recipe Tart Dough (see basic recipes)*

*1 egg*

1. Preheat the oven to 350°F.
2. Prepare the tart dough (see basic recipes).
3. Put the cream, sugar, corn syrup, and liqueurs in a saucepan. Bring to a boil, and reduce by half. Carefully regulate the heat to maintain a steady boil but avoid boilover. As it approaches completion, the mixture will take on a golden color; a rubber spatula drawn across the pan will leave a trail, exposing the bottom of the pan. When the mixture reaches this point, test it by dropping a small portion on a cool work surface. If it becomes quite firm when cool, the mixture is ready. Do not overcook, as the sugar will crystallize.
4. Pour this hot mixture over the walnuts and stir thoroughly with a rubber spatula until the mixture is uniform. Allow to cool. You can refrigerate this for several days if necessary.
5. Using a pastry cloth, roll out half of the tart dough into a circle and press it into a 10-inch tart pan with a removable bottom. Add the filling. Roll out the other half of the dough and place it on top, carefully sealing the edges together.
6. Beat the egg with a little water and apply this egg wash across the top of the pie with a pastry brush. Using the back of a fork, etch parallel lines lightly across the entire surface of the dough with the tines. Turn the pie 90 degrees and repeat, covering the top with a pattern of tiny squares.
7. Bake 45 minutes or until the top is golden brown. Allow to cool thoroughly.

# Appeltaart

This is not a misspelling, it's Dutch. Of the European languages, Dutch is most similar to English. The Dutch people are a beautiful and healthy lot who love food and have a refreshing outlook on life. This tart is a modification of the Dutch buttercake called *boterkoek*. It shows the Indonesian influence on Dutch cuisine through the use of candied ginger in the dough and is a good example of the use of copious amounts of butter typical of Dutch cuisine.

*4 ounces unsalted butter, chilled*

*1 cup all-purpose flour*

*3/4 cup sugar*

*1 tablespoon ginger, preserved in syrup (found in oriental markets)*

*2 tart apples, such as Granny Smith*

*3 eggs*

*1/2 cup heavy cream*

*a pinch grated nutmeg*

*1/4 cup apple jelly*

1.   Preheat the oven to 350°F.

2.   Cut the butter into the flour using a pastry knife, as in making pie dough. Stir 1/2 cup of the sugar in with a spoon.

3.   Chop the ginger fine and add it to the mixture. Separate the eggs and add one yolk, forming the mixture into a ball. Refrigerate the dough at least one hour.

4.   Peel, core, and slice the apples into thin wedges (see Appendix II-3).

5.   In a mixing bowl, beat one egg with one egg yolk and the remaining sugar. (Save the two remaining whites to use in another recipe.) Add the cream and stir by hand with a wire whip. Add the nutmeg and stir. This will be the custard filling.

6.   Using a pastry cloth, roll out the dough and press it into a 10-inch tart pan with a removable bottom. Trim the edges. Arrange the apple

slices in a pinwheel fashion, overlapping them, starting at the perimeter. Create a second, interior pinwheel arrangement, going in the reverse direction.

7.    Pour the custard around the edge of the tart first, allowing it to fill toward the center. Do not overfill. The apple slices should not be totally submerged in custard; let the pattern of apples show through.

8.    Bake for thirty minutes or until the edge of the crust is starting to brown. Allow to cool.

9.    Warm the apple jelly in a microwave oven or in the top of a double boiler over simmering water until thin and hot. Using a pastry brush, glaze the surface with the jelly, covering it completely. Allow it to set for ten minutes.

# Jalapeño Pecan Pie

As outrageous as it sounds, this is a terrific pie and truly Texas inspired. I candy the jalapeños, puree them, and add them to the richest possible pecan pie filling. Add a little or a lot—you be the judge. I add some of the pepper puree and then taste, looking for a pronounced jalapeño flavor and just a slight burn in the back of my mouth. Serve it with a scoop of Blue Bell® vanilla ice cream to complete the Texas motif (and to cut the heat generated by the jalapeños). After candying the peppers, save the syrup for experimentation with pancakes or such savories as barbecue sauce, pork loin marinade, and Asian dishes.

*2 cups sugar*

*1 cup water*

*6 fresh jalapeño peppers*

*1 cup light corn syrup*

*1 cup dark brown sugar*

*1 tablespoon vanilla extract*

*8 ounces unsalted butter, melted*

*4 eggs*

*2 tablespoons all-purpose flour*
*1/2 recipe Pâté Brisé (see basic recipes)*
*1 cup pecan halves*

1.    Preheat the oven to 350°F.

2.    Shell pecans if necessary, being careful to remove any small bits of shell or membrane.

3.    Prepare the pâté brisé (see basic recipes).

4.    Add one cup of sugar to the water in a heavy saucepan. Bring it to a boil.

5.    Slice the jalapeños in half lengthwise and add them to the developing syrup. *Be careful not to touch your eyes after handling the peppers, or use rubber gloves. Searing volatile oils will be given off with the rising steam, so stand back.* Cover if necessary. Allow to simmer for one-half hour or until the peppers are shriveled and dark. Remove them from the syrup and allow them to cool. Puree the peppers with a little of the syrup in a food processor or blender to form a paste.

6.    In a heavy saucepan bring the corn syrup, the remaining cup of sugar, the brown sugar, and vanilla to a boil, stirring occasionally. Remove the filling from the heat. Whisk in the melted butter until incorporated.

7.    Beat the eggs together in a bowl and pour them into the filling while whisking vigorously. Whisk in the flour.

8.    Strain the pie filling through a sieve to remove any coagulated egg. Allow the filling to stand a few minutes and skim any foam from the surface. Add the jalapeño puree a little at a time until the desired balance of flavor and heat is obtained.

9.    Roll out the pie dough and place it into a 9-inch foil pie pan. Pinch a decorative border along the edge. Place another pie pan inside and bake upside down for five minutes or until just starting to bake, having turned opaque, but not browned. (You can remove the top pan periodically to check for doneness.)

10.    Remove the interior pan, place the pecans in the bottom of the crust and add the filling. The pecans will rise to the top. Distribute them evenly across the surface of the pie. Return the pie to the oven and bake twenty minutes or until the filling is bubbling in the center and the crust is brown. Allow to cool completely. Refrigerate thoroughly for clean cutting.

# Bourbon Macadamia Pie

This pie is a derivative of the classic pecan pie, with macadamia nuts substituting for the pecans. Several liquors go well with pecan pie filling, bourbon and rum being two of my favorites. Change the nut back to pecan and use rum in this recipe and you have my favorite combination, the *rum pecan pie*.

The macadamia is native to Australia and is named after the scientist who promoted its cultivation, John MacAdam. Now grown commercially in Hawaii, this nut is costly, due—in part—to harvesting problems. Because it is difficult to tell when they are ripe, the nuts must be allowed to fall from the trees first and then be harvested by hand.

*1 cup light corn syrup*

*1 cup sugar*

*1 cup dark brown sugar*

*8 ounces unsalted butter, melted*

*4 eggs*

*2 tablespoons all-purpose flour*

*1 tablespoon bourbon*

*1/2 recipe Pâté Brisé (see basic recipes)*

*1 cup macadamia nuts, unsalted*

1. Preheat the oven to 350°F.
2. Prepare the pâté brisé (see basic recipes).
3. In a heavy saucepan bring the corn syrup, the sugar, and the brown sugar to a boil, stirring occasionally. Remove the filling from the heat. Whisk in the melted butter until incorporated.
4. Beat the eggs together in a bowl and pour them into the filling while whisking vigorously. Whisk in the flour.
5. Strain the pie filling through a sieve to remove any coagulated egg. Allow the filling to stand for a few minutes and skim any foam that has formed on the surface. Add the bourbon and stir with the mixer on low speed.

**6.** Using a pastry cloth, roll out the pie dough and place it into a 9-inch foil pie pan. Pinch a decorative border along the edge. Place another pie pan inside the pie dough and bake upside down for five minutes or until just starting to bake, having turned opaque, but not brown. (You can remove the top pan periodically to check for doneness.)

**7.** Remove the interior pan, place the macadamias in the bottom of the crust and add the filling. The nuts will rise to the top. Distribute them evenly across the surface of the pie. Return the pie to the oven and bake twenty minutes or until the filling is bubbling in the center and the crust is brown. Allow to cool completely. Refrigerate thoroughly for clean cutting.

# Fudge Pecan Pie

As if pecan pie were not rich enough, here's a version that has a chocolate fudge texture and flavor. It's like a candy bar with nuts, caramel, and chocolate all mixed together. Actually, that sounds pretty good!

*1 cup light corn syrup*

*1 cup sugar*

*1 cup dark brown sugar*

*1 tablespoon vanilla extract*

*8 ounces unsalted butter, melted*

*4 eggs*

*1/2 cup Chocolate Base (see basic recipes)*

*1/2 recipe Pâté Brisé (see basic recipes)*

*1 cup pecan halves*

**1.** Preheat the oven to 350°F.

**2.** Prepare the pâté brisé (see basic recipes).

**3.** Shell pecans if necessary, being careful to remove any small bits of shell or membrane.

**4.** Prepare the chocolate base (see basic recipes).

**5.** In a heavy saucepan bring the corn syrup, the sugar, the brown sugar, and vanilla to a boil, stirring occasionally. Remove the filling from the heat. Whisk in the melted butter until incorporated.

**6.** Beat the eggs together in a bowl and pour them into the filling while whisking vigorously.

**7.** Strain the pie filling through a sieve to remove any coagulated egg. Allow the filling to stand for a few minutes and skim any foam that has formed on the surface. Add the chocolate base and stir to blend.

**8.** Using a pastry cloth, roll out the pie dough and place it into a 9-inch foil pie pan. Pinch a decorative border along the edge. Place another pie pan inside and bake upside down for five minutes or until just starting to bake, having turned opaque, but not browned. (You can remove the top pan periodically to check for doneness.)

**9.** Remove the interior pan, place the pecans in the bottom of the crust and add the filling. The pecans will slowly rise to the top. Distribute them evenly across the surface of the pie. Return the pie to the oven and bake twenty minutes or until the filling is set in the center and the crust is brown. Allow to cool completely. Refrigerate thoroughly for clean cutting.

# Apple Chèvre Pie

My dad always liked a slice of cheese on his apple pie. As a kid I thought that was a perfectly good way to ruin a decent dessert. Was that a fifties thing? You don't hear about it much anymore. If you think about it, though, the sweetness of the pie *should* be balanced by the sharper taste of cheese. And so this pie was born. The tanginess of chèvre and the sweetness of an old-fashioned apple pie are great together, and this is a good way to feature another of Texas's quality ingredients—goat cheese. While it is produced across the state, my favorite is from Dripping Springs. Larsons Farms produces a wonderful Texas chèvre.

> *5 tart apples, such as Granny Smith*
> *1 cup sugar*
> *1 tablespoon cornstarch*
> *2 teaspoons ground cinnamon*
> *1 teaspoon ground allspice*
> *1 recipe (see basic recipes)*
> *2 ounces chèvre*

1.  Preheat the oven to 350°F.
2.  Prepare the pâté brisé (see basic recipes).
3.  Peel, core, and cut the apples into good-sized chunks (see Appendix II-3).
4.  Toss them with the sugar, cornstarch, and spices. As you toss them, the apples will release some juice and bind everything together.
5.  Using a pastry cloth, roll out half of the dough and place it into a 9-inch pie pan. Have the edge hang over the pan. Add the apple mixture and crumble the goat cheese over the surface.
6.  Roll out the other half of the dough and cut it into half-inch strips. Weave the strips into a lattice top. Join the lattice strips to the edge of the bottom crust and fold under. Pinch an attractive border with your fingers, a fork, or pie crimpers, if you have them.
7.  Bake for about an hour or until the filling is bubbling in the middle of the pie. Allow to cool.

# Double Fudge Chocolate Cream Pie

As an experienced baker, I have hundreds of cake recipes to choose from when I want to make my birthday cake. For the last ten birthdays I've made myself this pie. I guess it represents my childhood and my mom, and is therefore the perfect comfort food as I celebrate the aging process. When we ate at the diner I would often order chocolate cream pie (when they were out of blueberry) and quickly learned the subtleties of nomenclature. Imagine my horror on one occasion when the keenly anticipated chocolate pie I had ordered arrived topped with *meringue*. Whipped cream belongs on chocolate pie and meringue on lemon!

This is no ordinary chocolate pudding pie . . . the addition of a half-pound of Belgian chocolate sees to that.

> 1/2 *Pâté Brisé (see basic recipes)*
> 2 *cups heavy cream*
> 1 *cup milk*
> 5 *egg yolks*
> 3/4 *cup sugar*
> 1/4 *cup cocoa powder*
> 1/4 *cup cornstarch*
> 8 *ounces bittersweet chocolate (additional for garnish)*

1. Preheat the oven to 350°F.
2. Prepare the pâté brisé (see basic recipes).
3. Roll out the dough and place it into a 9-inch pie pan. Pinch a decorative border with your fingers. Set another pie pan on top of the rolled dough, invert, and bake upside down for ten minutes. (You can remove the top pan periodically to check for doneness.) Remove it from the oven, turn it right side up, remove the interior pan, and return the pie crust to the oven to continue baking. Remove the crust from the oven when golden in the center, as well as along the edge.

**4.**   Scald one cup of the cream with the milk in a heavy saucepan.

**5.**   Beat the egg yolks thoroughly with one-half cup of sugar, until the yolks are pale and thick. Add the cocoa and cornstarch and whisk to blend.

**6.**   Melt the chocolate in a microwave at low power or in the top of a double boiler over simmering water.

**7.**   Using a wire whip, stir the hot milk mixture into the egg yolk mixture until smooth. Return all of this to the saucepan and cook over medium heat until thickened and just beginning to boil.

**8.**   Stir in the melted chocolate until smooth and shiny. Add this filling to the baked pie crust. Cover with plastic wrap and refrigerate one hour minimum.

**9.**   Whip the remaining cream and sugar until stiff (see Appendix II–5). Top the pie with the whipped cream, either with a spatula or a pastry bag fitted with a large star tip, piping rosettes and shells to cover. Shave some chocolate over the top to garnish.

# ► CHEESECAKES ◄

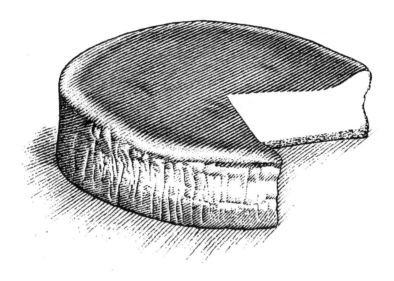

- ▶ Manhattan Cheesecake

- ▶ Pecan Acres Pumpkin Pecan Cheesecake

- ▶ Macadamia White Chocolate Cheesecake

- ▶ Frangelico Cheesecake

- ▶ Italian Cheesecake

- ▶ Mission Citrus Cheesecake

- ▶ Raspberry Harlequin Cheesecake

# Manhattan Cheesecake

With so many styles and flavors to choose from, cheesecake becomes a very personal matter. I have some strong opinions concerning cheese-cake. Texture is the fundamental polarizing property. I believe that the world is divided into two camps on this matter. On the one hand we have the smooth, soft, creamy camp who prefer what I believe is re-ferred to as "French style"; on the other, the firm, dryish, almost-impossible-to-swallow-without-a-glass-of-milk-in-my-other-hand camp who stand up for the New York style. I belong to the latter group, probably because I was raised in "the city," where you never visited anyone without bringing a cheesecake from your favorite neighbor-hood bakery.

I have another strong opinion concerning cheesecake and that re-gards the crust. A proper crust is of the baked, soft cookie style, not one made from smashed graham crackers. This recipe is a derivative of the cheesecake served at Lindy's, a Brooklyn landmark known for hav-ing one of the very best cheesecakes New York ever produced.

> 2 1/2 pounds cream cheese, at room temperature
> 1 2/3 cups sugar
> 1 tablespoon vanilla extract
> 1 teaspoon almond extract
> 2/3 cup cream, at room temperature
> 8 eggs, at room temperature
> 1 recipe Cheesecake Crust (see basic recipes)

1. Take the cream cheese, cream, and eggs from the refrigerator at least thirty minutes before they will be needed.
2. Preheat the oven to 350°F.
3. Prepare a parchment-lined 10-inch springform pan (see Appen-dix II–1).
4. Prepare cheesecake crust (see basic recipes).

5.  With an electric mixer, beat the cream cheese, sugar, and extracts together for three minutes or until the sugar is dissolved completely.

6.  With the mixer on low speed, gradually add the cream and stir for two minutes until the mixture is blended and smooth.

7.  Add the eggs, one at a time, waiting for each to be completely incorporated before adding the next.

8.  With a rubber spatula, scrape the sides of the bowl and mix one minute more.

9.  Using a pastry cloth, roll out the crust dough to about the diameter of the parchment-lined springform pan, set pan on the dough, and cut out a circle. Place the dough in the pan and press it in so that the dough is firmly against the edge of the pan. Bake until just brown in the center. Remove from oven and turn oven temperature down to 275°F.

10.  Pour the batter into the baked crust and bake at 275°F until set in the middle, about two hours. For a professional look, brown the top quickly under a broiler. Allow to cool, then chill overnight. Remove the cheesecake from the pan and peel off the parchment. Keep refrigerated until ready to serve.

▼

# Pecan Acres Pumpkin Pecan Cheesecake

◇

On the banks of the Brazos river lies Pecan Acres ranch, the home of Vernon and Dotie Frost. Mr. Frost is a true patriarch and a Texas classic. An oil wildcatter in the twenties, he has been a rancher for over fifty years. His hobby is raising pecans, and with over 1,000 acres of manicured pecan groves, it is quite a hobby. He has always treated me like family whenever I've had the pleasure of visiting the ranch, and I always try to bring him his favorite dessert, not a pecan pie, surprisingly, but a Manhattan cheesecake! In his honor and to celebrate a perfect fall combination, I have created this special dessert.

2 *pounds cream cheese, at room temperature*

1 2/3 *cups sugar*

2/3 *cup cream, at room temperature*

8 *eggs, at room temperature*

1 *15-ounce can pumpkin (not pie filling)*

1 *tablespoon pumpkin pie spice (cinnamon, allspice, and ginger)*

1 *recipe Cheesecake Crust (see basic recipes)*

2 *ounces pecan halves, none broken*

1.   Take the cream cheese, cream, and eggs from the refrigerator at least thirty minutes before they will be needed.

2.   Shell pecans if necessary, being careful to remove any small bits of shell or membrane.

3.   Preheat the oven to 350°F.

4.   Prepare a parchment-lined 10-inch springform pan (see Appendix II–1).

5.   Prepare cheesecake crust (see basic recipes).

6.   With the electric mixer, beat the cream cheese and sugar together for three minutes or until the sugar is completely dissolved.

7.   Gradually add the cream and stir for two minutes with the mixer on low speed. Scrape down the mixing bowl with a rubber spatula and mix thirty seconds more.

8.   Add the eggs, one at a time, waiting for each to be completely incorporated before adding the next. Scrape down the bowl and stir thirty seconds more.

9.   Place the pumpkin in a small bowl and stir in the spice mixture. Add a small ladle of the cream cheese mixture and stir it in.

10.   Add this pumpkin mixture to the cream cheese mixture and stir one minute.

11.   Using a pastry cloth, roll out the crust dough to about the diameter of the parchment-lined springform pan, set the pan on the dough, and cut out a circle. Place the dough in the pan and press it in so that the dough is firmly against the edge of the pan. Bake until just brown in the center. Remove pan from oven and turn oven temperature down to 275°F.

**12.** Pour the cheesecake batter into the baked crust. Place pecan halves around the outside edge of the cheesecake, being careful to have all pecans oriented in the same way (I like to have them "good side" up with the pointy end toward the center). Continue with a second row. Repeat until entire surface is covered with pecans.

**13.** Bake at 275°F until set in the middle, about two hours. Allow to cool, and refrigerate overnight. Remove the cheesecake from the pan and peel off the parchment. Keep refrigerated until ready to serve.

# Macadamia White Chocolate Cheesecake

With two of the most expensive ingredients that you could add to a dessert, this recipe may be dismissed as a predictable attempt to curry favor with trendy food types. Nothing could be further from the truth . . . these are wonderful additions to a cheesecake and act in perfect harmony with the inherent flavors of the basic Manhattan recipe. The macadamias are pan-roasted and take on a special personality. White chocolate, which isn't really chocolate at all, is the only "chocolate" that should ever be added to a cheesecake. If you truly love chocolate, have a chocolate dessert or nibble on a block of quality couverture, but never add it to a cheesecake. The flavors of the cheesecake work in opposition to the subtleties of fine chocolate. Test your friends . . . if they say that they love chocolate cheesecake, they are not discriminating chocoholics!

*2 ounces macadamia nuts, raw*

*2 pounds cream cheese, at room temperature*

*1 2/3 cups sugar*

*1 1/2 tablespoons vanilla extract*

*2/3 cup cream, at room temperature*
*8 eggs, at room temperature*
*8 ounces high-quality white chocolate*
*1 recipe Cheesecake Crust (see basic recipes )*

1.    Take the cream cheese, cream, and eggs from the refrigerator at least thirty minutes before they will be needed.

2.    Preheat the oven to 350°F.

3.    Prepare a parchment-lined 10-inch springform pan (see Appendix II – 1).

4.    Prepare cheesecake crust (see basic recipes).

5.    Heat a heavy, nonstick skillet and add the macadamia nuts. Constantly swirl the pan to keep the nuts moving. Carefully toast the nuts until browned but not burned. Allow to cool. Chop the nuts coarsely.

6.    With the electric mixer, beat the cream cheese, sugar, and vanilla together for three minutes or until the sugar is dissolved completely.

7.    With the mixer on low speed, gradually add the cream and stir for two minutes until the mixture is blended and smooth.

8.    Add the eggs, one at a time, waiting for each to be completely incorporated before adding the next.

9.    With a rubber spatula, scrape the sides of the bowl and mix one minute more.

10.    Melt the white chocolate in the top of a double boiler over simmering water or carefully in a microwave oven at low power. Stir the chocolate into the batter.

11.    Using a pastry cloth, roll out the crust dough to about the diameter of the parchment-lined springform pan, set the pan on the dough, and cut out a circle. Place the dough in the pan and press it in so that the dough is firmly against the edge of the pan. Bake until just brown in the center. Remove pan from oven and turn oven temperature down to 275°F.

12.    Pour the cheesecake batter into the baked crust. Sprinkle the top with the chopped, toasted macadamias and bake at 275°F until set in the middle, about two hours. Allow to cool and refrigerate overnight. Remove the cheesecake from the pan and peel off the parchment. Keep refrigerated until ready to serve.

# Frangelico Cheesecake

I look for any excuse to use hazelnuts in a recipe. When I can also include hazelnut liqueur, Frangelico, all the better. This recipe has both. While we are talking about hazelnuts, I thank God that someone had the wisdom to create an alternative name to *filbert*. The Italians wisely referred to the filbert as *nocciola* and the French followed suit with *noisette*. Can you imagine a "filbert torte"?

*2 ounces hazelnuts (filberts)*

*2 1/2 pounds cream cheese, at room temperature*

*1 2/3 cups sugar*

*1 tablespoon vanilla extract*

*1/2 cup cream, at room temperature*

*8 eggs, at room temperature*

*1/4 cup Frangelico liqueur*

*1 recipe Cheesecake Crust (see basic recipes)*

**1.** Take the cream cheese, cream, and eggs from the refrigerator at least thirty minutes before they will be needed.

**2.** Preheat the oven to 350°F.

**3.** Prepare a parchment-lined 10-inch springform pan (see Appendix II–1).

**4.** Prepare hazelnuts (see Appendix II–4).

**5.** Prepare cheesecake crust (see basic recipes).

**6.** With an electric mixer beat the cream cheese, sugar, and extracts together for three minutes or until the sugar is dissolved completely.

**7.** With the mixer on low speed, gradually add the cream and stir for two minutes until the mixture is blended and smooth.

**8.** Add the eggs, one at a time, waiting for each to be completely incorporated before adding the next.

**9.** With a rubber spatula, scrape the sides of the bowl and mix one minute more.

**10.**    Stir in the Frangelico.

**11.**    Using a pastry cloth, roll out the crust dough to about the diameter of the parchment-lined springform pan, set the pan on the dough, and cut out a circle. Place the dough in the pan and press it in so that the dough is firmly against the edge of the pan. Bake until just brown in the center. Remove pan from oven and turn oven temperature down to 275°F.

**12.**    Pour the cheesecake batter into the baked crust. Sprinkle the top with the chopped, toasted hazelnuts and bake at 275°F until set in the middle, about two hours. Allow to cool and refrigerate overnight. Remove the cheesecake from the pan and peel off the parchment. Keep refrigerated until ready to serve.

# Italian Cheesecake

I have no idea whether or not this cheesecake is actually made in Italy, but it *is* based on ricotta rather than cream cheese. A great Italian bakery in New York produced such a cake, and one of my all-time favorite restaurants—The Canal House—served a cake like this in the 1970s. In Texas many people enjoy a rich dessert after an Italian meal, and this cake will do nicely.

> *2 pounds Frigo® ricotta cheese, whole milk*
> *preferred, at room temperature*
>
> *1/2 cup sugar*
>
> *2 teaspoons vanilla extract*
>
> *2 tablespoons all-purpose flour*
>
> *8 egg yolks, at room temperature*
>
> *1 cup cream, at room temperature*
>
> *1 tablespoon orange curaçao or Grand Marnier*
>
> *1 recipe Cheesecake Crust (see basic recipes)*

**1.** If the ricotta contains excess liquid, drain it in a cheesecloth-lined strainer for two hours.

**2.** Take the ricotta, cream, and eggs from the refrigerator at least thirty minutes before they will be needed.

**3.** Preheat the oven to 350°F.

**4.** Prepare a parchment-lined 10-inch springform pan (see Appendix II-1).

**5.** Prepare cheesecake crust (see basic recipes).

**6.** Mix the ricotta, sugar, and vanilla with an electric mixer for two minutes or until the sugar is completely dissolved.

**7.** With the mixer on low speed, add the flour and stir in. Add the egg yolks, one at a time, and stir until smooth. Scrape down the sides of the bowl and mix thirty seconds more.

**8.** Add the cream and the orange liqueur of your choice. Stir to blend.

**9.** Using a pastry cloth, roll out the crust dough to about the diameter of the parchment-lined springform pan, set the pan on the dough, and cut out a circle. Place the dough in the pan and press it in so that the dough is firmly against the edge of the pan. Bake until just brown in the center. Remove pan from oven and turn oven temperature down to 325°F.

**10.** Pour the batter into the baked crust and bake in a 325°F oven until it is golden brown and the top is just beginning to crack, about one-and-a-half hours.

**11.** Allow the cake to cool and refrigerate several hours (or overnight). Remove the cheesecake from the pan and peel off the parchment. Keep refrigerated until ready to serve.

# Mission Citrus Cheesecake

◇

◇

The Rio Grande Valley produces citrus that rivals the best that California and Florida have to offer. Edinburg, Mission, Pharr, and Rio Hondo offer oranges, lemons, grapefruits, and limes of the highest quality. "The Valley," as it is known, isn't really a valley at all. It's a giant floodplain for the Rio Grande River, but I guess some of the romanticism would be lost if we had to refer to the fine produce that "the floodplain" had to offer. Lemon flavors the cheesecake batter and the cake can be topped with your choice: tequila-marinated orange slices or candied orange slices (for those who prefer an alcohol-free dessert).

◇

*For the marinated orange slices:*
*2 medium oranges*
*1 cup tequila, preferably a high-quality añejo type*

1.   Carefully peel the oranges, removing the pith as well. Slice them as thinly as possible.
2.   Arrange the slices in a shallow pan and pour the tequila over them. Cover with plastic wrap and refrigerate for several hours.
3.   Thoroughly drain the orange slices and save the tequila (it's wonderful in margaritas!).

*For the candied orange slices:*
*2 medium oranges, washed thoroughly*
*2 cups water*
*2 cups sugar*

1.   Prepare the simple syrup by adding the sugar to the center of a heavy saucepan containing the water. Place on high heat and allow the mixture to come to a boil. Do not stir the developing syrup at any time. Reduce the heat to a simmer.
2.   Slice the oranges as thinly as possible and add them to the syrup. Continue to simmer for one hour. Allow to cool and stand, covered, overnight. Return the pan to the heat and simmer one hour. Allow to cool and stand again, covered, overnight.
3.   Drain the orange slices and reserve the syrup for another use.

*For the cheesecake:*
*2 1/2 pounds cream cheese, at room temperature*
*1 2/3 cups sugar*
*1 tablespoon vanilla extract*
*2 tablespoons lemon juice, freshly squeezed*
*2/3 cup cream, at room temperature*
*8 eggs, at room temperature*
*1 tablespoon lemon zest*
*1 recipe Cheesecake Crust (see basic recipes)*

1. Choose marinated or candied orange slices and make a day ahead.

2. Take the cream cheese, cream, and eggs from the refrigerator at least thirty minutes before they will be needed.

3. Preheat the oven to 350°F.

4. Prepare a parchment-lined 10-inch springform pan (see Appendix II–1).

5. Prepare cheesecake crust (see basic recipes).

6. With an electric mixer beat the cream cheese, sugar, vanilla, and lemon juice together for three minutes or until the sugar is dissolved completely.

7. With the mixer on low speed, gradually add the cream and stir for two minutes until the mixture is blended and smooth.

8. Add the eggs, one at a time, waiting for each to be completely incorporated before adding the next. Add the lemon zest.

9. With a rubber spatula, scrape the sides of the bowl and mix one minute more.

10. Using a pastry cloth, roll out the crust dough to about the diameter of the parchment-lined springform pan, set the pan on the dough and cut out a circle. Place the dough in the pan and press it in so that the dough is firmly against the edge of the pan. Bake at 350°F until just brown in the center. Remove pan from oven and turn oven temperature down to 275°F.

11. Pour cheesecake batter into baked crust and bake at 275°F until set in the middle, about two hours. Allow to cool and refrigerate overnight. Remove the cheesecake from the pan and peel off the parchment.

12. Arrange orange slices in an overlapping manner to cover the top of the cheesecake. Keep refrigerated until ready to serve.

# Raspberry Harlequin Cheesecake

Fruit and cheesecake make a classic combination. Topping with straw-berries, blueberries, or pineapple is an excellent way to serve the Man-hattan cheesecake, but in this version the berries are incorporated with part of the batter and then swirled into the cake. Fresh raspberries are best; in Texas the small town of Brownsboro grows a tasty variety.

> 2 1/2 pounds cream cheese, at room temperature
> 1 2/3 cups sugar
> 1 tablespoon vanilla extract
> 2/3 cup cream, at room temperature
> 1 tablespoon Chambord or other raspberry liqueur
> 8 eggs, at room temperature
> 6 ounces fresh raspberries (frozen will do if necessary)
> 1 recipe Cheesecake Crust (see basic recipes)

1. Take the cream cheese, cream, and eggs from the refrigerator at least thirty minutes before they will be needed.

2. Preheat the oven to 350°F.

3. Prepare a parchment-lined 10-inch springform pan (see Appendix II–1).

4. Prepare cheesecake crust (see basic recipes).

5. With an electric mixer beat the cream cheese, sugar, and vanilla together for three minutes or until the sugar is dissolved completely.

6. Gradually add the cream and stir for two minutes with the mixer on low speed until the mixture is blended and smooth. Add the rasp-berry liqueur.

7. Add the eggs, one at a time, waiting for each to be completely in-corporated before adding the next.

8. With a rubber spatula, scrape the sides of the bowl and mix one minute more.

9. Puree the raspberries in a blender. Push the mixture through a fine sieve with a rubber spatula to remove the seeds. With a wire whip, stir in one cup of the cheesecake mixture until homogeneous.

10. Using a pastry cloth, roll out the crust dough to about the diameter of the parchment-lined springform pan, set the pan on the dough and cut out a circle. Place the dough in the pan and press it in so that the dough is firmly against the edge of the pan. Bake at 350°F until just brown in the center. Remove pan from oven and turn oven temperature down to 275°F.

11. Add half of the cheesecake batter to the pan. Drop half-ounce (1 tablespoon) dollops of the raspberry mixture on the surface. Using the point of a small, sharp knife, swirl the raspberry mixture into the batter. Do not completely mix the two; rather allow for distinct regions of the raspberry and cheesecake batters.

12. Carefully ladle the remaining cheesecake batter onto the surface. Add dollops of raspberry mixture in a checkerboard pattern on the top. Swirl with a clean knife point or skewer so as to "feather" the edges between the two batters.

13. Bake at 275°F until set in the middle, about two hours. Allow to cool and refrigerate overnight. Remove the cake from the pan and peel off the parchment. Keep refrigerated until ready to serve.

# ▸ OTHER DESSERTS ◂

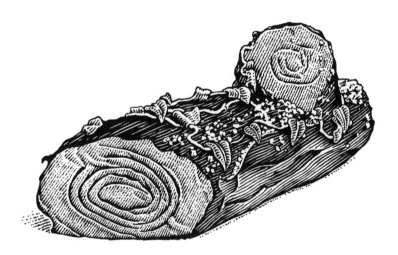

- Chocolate Terrine with Ginger Crème Anglaise

- Huajillo Honey Mango Rum Bread Pudding with Caramel Sauce

- Thai Coconut Custard Cake

- Fresh Strawberry Napoleons

- Bûche de Noël

# Chocolate Terrine
# with Ginger Crème Anglaise

The most unusual request for a dessert from my bakery came from a chef brought to Austin from the Coyote Cafe in Santa Fe. Unusual because it was for a Chinese restaurant, which are not known for serving dessert other than the obligatory fortune cookie. Actually, the concept was Californian Chinoise and I guess that special desserts fit into that scheme. The ginger in the crème plays very nicely against the fruitiness of good chocolate. The "terrine" is an unbaked pâté, formed in the classic loaf shape and served in thick slices.

*1 1/2 pounds bittersweet chocolate*

*1 cup heavy cream*

*4 ounces unsalted butter*

*3 tablespoons orange juice concentrate*

*1 ounce shelled pistachio nuts*

*1 ounce fresh ginger root*

*1 cup milk*

*4 egg yolks*

*1/2 cup sugar*

*1 teaspoon vanilla extract*

*fruit puree or chocolate sauce (optional)*

1.    Prepare a 7-inch loaf pan by lining it with plastic wrap. Allow the plastic to overhang enough to cover the top when filled.

2.    Melt the chocolate in the top of a double boiler over simmering water or in a microwave oven at low power. Using a wire whip, stir in the cream, butter, and orange juice concentrate. Whisk until uniform and glossy.

3.    Fill the prepared loaf pan halfway with the chocolate mixture. Place the pistachios across the surface. Cover the nuts with the re-

maining chocolate mixture, filling the pan. Cover the top with the excess plastic wrap and refrigerate several hours.

4.  Prepare the crème anglaise by first peeling the ginger root and slicing it thinly. Add the ginger to the milk in a heavy saucepan. Scald the milk and then let it steep with the ginger for five minutes.

5.  Beat the egg yolks with the sugar and vanilla until pale and light. Add a little of the milk to the eggs and whisk. Using a wire whip, add the remaining milk and stir to blend. Return this mixture to the saucepan and cook over low heat until thickened and just beginning to simmer. Strain the custard through a fine sieve to remove the ginger and any coagulated egg. Cover with plastic and refrigerate until needed.

6.  To serve, ladle about one ounce of sauce in the center of the plate. Pick up the plate and tip it in all directions while rotating so that the sauce covers most of the surface. Place a slice of the chocolate terrine in the center. For added presentation, place drops of a fruit purée or chocolate sauce at several points on the custard around the terrine and draw the point of a sharp knife through the drops.

▼

# Huajillo Honey Mango Rum Bread Pudding with Caramel Sauce

◇

With a restaurant producing its own freshly baked breads daily, one always seems to have leftovers. Chefs can use only so many breadcrumbs and croutons, so it is imperative to find a good use for the leftover loaves of rustic Italian bread. This is it. You can use almost any leftover or stale bread except rye or other seeded/herbed varieties (we discovered some spectacular variations with pumpkin bread and banana bread, so feel free to be creative). The flowering huajillo shrub is the source of the recommended honey, but other honeys will work quite well, including two other Texas favorites—mesquite and wildflower. Dried mango has the necessary firm texture needed to maintain its integrity and provides a year-round solution to availability. Our adminis-

trative assistant at the university, who is from the bread pudding capital (New Orleans ... pronounced "Nawlins"), tells me that bread pudding is a lot like cheesecake in that its evaluation is extremely subjec-
tive. According to her, this recipe does *not* resemble bread pudding in
texture but is more like a cake.

6 *ounces dried mango*

4 *ounces dark rum*

1-*pound loaf of bread, preferably a day or two old
and unsliced*

4 *cups heavy cream*

3 *eggs*

1 *cup sugar*

   *a pinch of nutmeg*

4 *ounces huajillo honey (other types are fine as well)*

1. Preheat the oven to 350°F.

2. Prepare a Pyrex® baking dish or casserole dish by applying a thin
layer of butter.

3. The caramel sauce can be made ahead if desired (see step 11).

4. In a microwave oven set at medium or in a small saucepan, heat the
dried mango in the rum for two minutes. Allow to stand until needed.
Remove the mango from the rum and save both.

5. Trim the crust from the bread and cut the loaf into half-inch slices.
Place one-third of the bread slices in the prepared baking dish, overlapping them, to cover the bottom completely.

6. Prepare a custard by whisking two cups of the cream, the eggs,
1/2 cup of sugar, and the rum together. Add the nutmeg. Pour approximately 1/3 of the custard over the bread, enough just to cover the
bread. Press down on the bread to aid in soaking up the custard.

7. Drizzle 2 ounces of the honey over the bread. Cover with half the
mango.

8. Add a second layer of bread and another third of the custard.
Press down to soak this layer. Drizzle the remaining honey over this
layer and cover with the rest of the mango. Add the final layer of bread
and the rest of the custard.

**9.** Cover the dish with foil and bake for twenty minutes. Remove the foil and continue to bake until golden and set in the center, about twenty more minutes. Allow to cool.

**10.** Cut into rectangles and serve as is, or warm the slices in a microwave oven. Top with powdered sugar and serve with caramel sauce (recipe follows).

**11.** For the caramel sauce, heat the remaining half-cup of sugar in a heavy saucepan or deep skillet over medium heat until the sugar has melted, has taken on an amber color, and is just beginning to smoke. Carefully add the remaining two cups of cream and whisk until incorporated. Continue to cook over medium heat until thickened, about two minutes. This sauce can be made ahead and warmed when needed.

# Thai Coconut Custard Cake

A very good friend of mine who is Thai owns three Thai restaurants. I studied up on Thai cuisine to try to develop a torte for him, but unfortunately, the Thai notion of dessert does not include the concept of cake. Custards and sweet rice dishes are popular, and coconut appears in many desserts as well. This torte features a baked coconut custard between two cake layers. The cake batter will remind the experienced baker of an Italian cream cake (mostly because it *is* a recipe for Italian cream cake minus the pecans). Toasted coconut garnishes the cake, which is frosted with a coconut-cream icing. This is the only one of my cakes that I've never tasted. I absolutely HATE coconut, although I've been told by some very reliable dessertaholics that it's quite delicious.

*2 cups heavy cream*

*8 eggs*

*1 can coconut cream (the type used in piña coladas)*

*2 cups sugar*

*1 pinch nutmeg*

*6 ounces unsalted butter, at room temperature*

*2 teaspoons vanilla extract*

*1 1/2 cups flour, all-purpose*

*1 teaspoon baking soda*

*3/4 cup buttermilk*

*1 cup shredded coconut, unsweetened*

*1/2 recipe Buttercream Base (see basic recipes)*

1.    Take the butter from the refrigerator at least thirty minutes before it will be needed.

2.    Preheat the oven to 350°F.

3.    Prepare three parchment-lined 9-inch round cake pans (see Appendix II–1).

4.    Using a wire whip, prepare the custard layer by combining the cream, four eggs, half of the coconut cream, one-half cup of sugar, and the nutmeg in a bowl.

5.    Pour the custard into one of the parchment-lined cake pans. Set it in a larger pan. Pour hot water into the larger pan to form a *bain-marie*, with enough water to come halfway up the sides of the custard pan. Bake until the custard is just set in the middle, about ten minutes. Allow to cool.

6.    Separate the remaining eggs and whip the whites in the electric mixer with 1/2 cup of sugar until firm, glossy peaks form.

7.    Using the mixer, and in a separate bowl, cream the butter with the remaining sugar. Add the egg yolks and vanilla and beat thirty seconds. Scrape down the bowl and beat one minute more.

8.    Sift the flour with the baking soda and add it gradually to the butter mixture, alternating with the buttermilk. Scrape down the bowl and stir until smooth. With the mixer on very low speed so as not to "splash," stir in half the shredded coconut.

9.    Bake in the two remaining parchment-lined cake pans for twenty minutes, or until firm to the touch in the center. Allow to cool.

10.    Toast the remaining shredded coconut in the oven until browned.

11.    Prepare buttercream base (see basic recipes).

12.    Beat the buttercream base with the remaining coconut cream. This can be done either with the mixer or by hand, as circumstances dictate.

13.    Assemble the cake by placing the baked custard on the first cake layer. Press the second cake layer on the custard. Trim the side of the cake with a serrated knife. Ice with the buttercream. Press the toasted coconut over the entire surface of the cake. Keep refrigerated until ready to serve.

# Fresh Strawberry Napoleons

Napoleons are usually made in a large sheet and then cut into small rectangles. A special form is used to aid in this process. Napoleons, which consist of layers of puff pastry, tend to break and shatter. In order to avoid this and to be able to include fresh fruit, I make "loose" napoleons, baking the puff pastry separately, already cut into individual servings. This allows for interesting shapes to the napoleons as well as for crisp pastry, since the fillings are added just before serving. I'm recommending the use of frozen puff pastry dough for ease (many commercial bakeries use it as well), although homemade is superior in flavor.

◇

*1 sheet frozen puff pastry dough*

*2 cups heavy cream*

*1 vanilla bean, sliced lengthwise*

*4 egg yolks*

*1/4 cup sugar*

*3 tablespoons cornstarch*

*2 tablespoons unsalted butter, at room temperature*

*1 cup Chocolate Base (see basic recipes)*

*1 pint fresh strawberries (other berries are fine)*

*chopped pistachios (optional)*

*chocolate vermicelli (optional)*

1.  Take the butter from the refrigerator at least thirty minutes before it will be needed.

2.  Preheat the oven to 400°F.

3.  Line a cookie sheet with parchment.

4.  Cut the puff pastry into six individual servings, using a cookie cutter or knife. (I use a Texas-shaped or a scalloped, round cutter.) Place them on the prepared cookie sheet and bake for fifteen minutes or until puffed and well browned. Allow to cool.

5.  Scald the cream in a heavy nonreactive saucepan with the vanilla bean. In a mixing bowl beat the yolks thoroughly with the sugar until pale and light. Using a wire whip, stir the cornstarch into the egg mixture to blend.

6.  Remove the vanilla bean from the cream and scrape the seeds from the pod into the cream. Add the cream, a little at a time, to the egg mixture while whisking. Return this mixture to the saucepan and cook over low heat until thickened and just starting to boil. Remove the pan from the heat and whisk mixture to release the steam. Pass through a sieve and stir in the butter. Cover with plastic wrap and allow to cool thoroughly.

7.  Prepare chocolate base (see basic recipes).

8.  Heat the chocolate base until it is melted and quite thin.

9.  Trim and slice the strawberries.

10.  To assemble the napoleons, cut each pastry laterally into thirds. Place the custard in a pastry bag fitted with a large star tip. Pipe custard onto the first pastry layer and top with slices of strawberries. Add the second pastry layer and repeat with custard and berries.

11.  Brush the top layer of puff pastry with melted chocolate base to cover completely, using a pastry brush. Set the tops on each napoleon. Garnish with chopped pistachios, chocolate vermicelli, etc.

# Bûche de Noël

Traditionally, in many French homes, a special log is burned on Christmas Eve. This dessert represents the Yule log and is decorated accordingly. Typically it is a rolled cake (like a jelly roll) which is made to look like a log with frostings and special garnishes such as meringue "mushrooms." I wanted my cake to be layered like a torte rather than rolled, but how to form it into a cylinder? I used a technique that I had discovered when a customer had ordered a large cake in the shape of an open book. I tried in vain to get him to accept a closed book . . . *much* easier, but to no avail. As with most good ideas, it came to me in the middle of the night: Carve it! I had discovered cake sculpting. I froze the cake after filling it, and, using a very sharp serrated knife, carved it into the shape of an open book. I applied this technique to the bûche by first building a long, rectangular cake and freezing it solid. I then carefully shaved the corners and sculpted it into a log shape. The chocolate frosting was applied to look like bark, a chocolate buttercream vine "grew" over the log, chopped hazelnuts at the ends simulated sawdust and a final dusting of white chocolate "snow" finished the presentation.

> *1 recipe Basic Chocolate Cake (see basic recipes)*
> *1 pound bittersweet chocolate*
> *1 recipe Buttercream Base (see basic recipes)*
> *2 fluid ounces orange curaçao or Chambord*
> *1 cup Chocolate Base, at room temperature (see basic recipes)*
> *White chocolate shavings*

1. Preheat the oven to 350°F.
2. Prepare a parchment-lined half-sheet (12-by-16-by-1-inch) pan (see Appendix II–1).
3. Prepare chocolate base (see basic recipes) and refrigerate until thick and spreadable.
4. Prepare basic chocolate cake (see basic recipes).
5. Bake the cake in the parchment-lined half-sheet pan for fifteen

minutes or until firm to the touch in the center. Allow to cool. Trim the edges and cut into four 4-by-12-inch rectangles.

6. Prepare buttercream base (see basic recipes).

7. Melt the chocolate in the top of a double boiler over simmering water or in a microwave oven at low power. With an electric mixer, beat the chocolate into the buttercream base. Scrape down the sides of the bowl and, with the mixer on low speed, stir until uniform.

8. Sprinkle the first cake layer with liqueur and spread a layer of buttercream over it. Add the second cake layer and repeat with liqueur and buttercream. Repeat with the third layer. Top with the fourth cake layer. With a spatula, press buttercream into the sides of the cake to eliminate any gaps. Freeze thoroughly, preferably overnight.

9. Remove the cake from the freezer and sculpt it into a log shape with a sharp, serrated knife. Start by removing the corners and work your way around. The bottom can be a bit flat, but the top should be nicely rounded. Cut each end off diagonally. Save these pieces for adding to the cake to simulate a knot or cut branch.

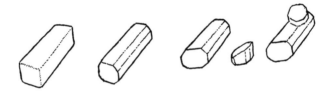

10. Using a little buttercream as "glue," attach one of the trimmed edges to the upper side of the cake, near one end. Ice the complete cake with chocolate buttercream, including all ends. With the tines of a fork, make concentric circles on each end to simulate rings of growth. Reserve the remaining buttercream for decoration. Place the cake in the freezer until the buttercream is hard.

11. Ice the cake with the chocolate base, making the frosting look like bark by using random, parallel motions with the spatula. Do not ice the ends.

12. Using a pastry bag fitted with a small, plain tip and a leaf tip, pipe a vine of buttercream growing around the log. Shave some white chocolate, using a grater, over one side of the cake to simulate snow. Keep refrigerated until ready to serve.

# Appendix I

## *Icing and Decorating Techniques*

◇

◇

After you have baked the cake and made the filling and frosting, assembly is next. With just a few tools and tricks, your cake can look luscious. But first, a caveat: do not expect the finished product to look like something out of a magazine or cake decorating book. It will not. It cannot! The people who produce those perfect photographs of perfect cakes are misleading you. Have you noticed that the cakes in the decorating magazines are perfectly shaped? Do you know why? Rather than ice an actual cake, they often frost the inverted metal cake pan and then decorate it! Personally, I don't like the look of perfection. There is something especially sensual about a cake that looks as though someone made it with their hands and heart. Not sloppy, mind you, but carefully prepared and possessing those minor imperfections that make it look handmade. I believe the line drawings of the cakes in this book convey this quality better than photographs would have done.

Let me start off by passing on the cardinal rule when it comes to icing and decorating. *Have lots of frosting.* After decorating thousands of cakes professionally, it's the most important thing that I can tell you. Whenever I've ruined a cake, it's been because I was trying to stretch that last bit of frosting to complete the cake. The tension generated by worrying whether there is enough frosting in the pastry bag to finish the decorative border is enough to ruin whatever border is being applied. Trying to save enough frosting for the decorative border results in spreading the sides too thin, ruins the shape of the cake, and allows crumbs and bare spots to show. Release yourself from these anxieties! Let your right brain flow with unshackled creativity! Have lots of frosting. (The recipes in the basics chapter provide more than enough frosting to ice any of the cakes in this book.)

### Filling Between the Layers

To fill between cake layers, place a large dollop of frosting in the center of the layer, and work your way to the edges. An offset spatula is best for establishing a level layer. Don't worry about getting the frosting all the way to the edges—they will be filled in from the sides. Press the top layer of cake firmly over the frosting layer, being careful to make the top layer level. With a spatula, spread some frosting around the sides, pressing in between the layers in order to fill in spaces left from stacking the cake layers together (see figure below). Spread a thin layer of frosting all around the sides of the cake. This is not the final frosting for the sides, but rather a "crumb layer." It will prevent any crumbs from showing through the final layer and allow for a smooth application of frosting all around the cake. If the cake is particularly crumbly, you might want to place some of your frosting in a small bowl for this crumb layer, to avoid introducing cake crumbs into your bulk frosting.

Spread generous amounts of frosting around the sides, then smooth the surface with your spatula, removing any excess. When smoothing and finishing a frosting layer, it is important to clean your spatula of frosting *after each use* to give a smooth appearance and prevent the "pulling up" of frosting already applied. Once the sides are spread to your satisfaction, smooth the top edge by using the offset spatula to spread excess frosting toward the center.

### Frosting the Top

Place a large dollop of frosting in the center of the top of the cake and spread the frosting to the edge of the cake, as you did for the filling layers, only this time spread the frosting so that it goes out past the top edge of the cake. Using a clean spatula, go around the sides and make a sharp edge to the cake by spreading the overhanging frosting to the center of the top of the cake. Use the offset spatula to smooth the top surface. This technique produces a smooth surface over the entire cake, making any decorative border work applied later stand out.

Occasionally the stacked layers are so unevenly aligned that trimming the sides becomes necessary. (It helps to chill the cake in the freezer for a while so that the layers do not slide around.) In any case, the sides of the cake layers are usually a bit more done than the interior, and it is a good idea to trim the sides. Do this with a sharp, serrated knife after filling the cake and before applying the crumb layer of frosting.

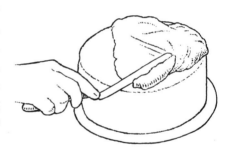

### Decorating the Cake

Decoration can be accomplished with a few simple techniques and tools. A metal spatula can give texture to the surface of your smoothly iced cake in the following ways. First, making peaks with frosting gives an old-fashioned look that is reminiscent of the way Mom iced her cakes in the fifties. To accomplish this, take a small amount of frosting on the end of your spatula, pressing it gently on the surface of the smoothly iced cake and pulling up from the top (or out from the sides) abruptly to form the peaks. Continue around the entire surface. Another spatula technique involves holding the edge and tip of the spatula at an angle to the surface of the smoothly iced cake. Moving the spatula up and down as you go around the sides of the cake produces an interesting pattern. Using a curved motion from the edge to the center of the top of the cake, going all around the circumference, makes a very nice surface (see figure), which I like to finish off by making a peak at the center intersection of all the lines.

Using a pastry bag with a decorative tip gives the finished cake a more formal look. Hundreds of tips are available to produce leaves, roses, lines, stars, and so on. The best way to learn about their uses is to take a class in cake decorating. Such instruction is beyond the scope of this book, so in this appendix I will discuss only the tip that can produce the most variety in borders and decoration—the star tip. It can make drop stars, rosettes, shell and scroll borders, and fleurs de lis. To make a rosette, hold the tip perpendicular to the surface and gently press out some frosting.

Proceed clockwise (or counterclockwise) in a tight circle (see above). Be sure to stop squeezing before lifting up to end the rosette; failure to do so is the most common mistake in tip work.

To make shells, hold the tip at a 45-degree angle to the surface and press gently. Lift slightly as you move back and down to complete the shell. The next shell will be placed over the ending portion of the last one, so don't worry about any rough edge to the end of a shell.

A cake comb can make very fine parallel ridges on the smoothed surfaces of an iced cake. It is a triangular device that makes a different

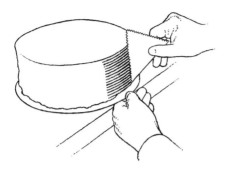

pattern on each of its sides. To use this tool properly, make sure that the comb is vertical when etching the sides and horizontal when used on top. Making wavy motions as you pass the comb across the top of a cake creates interesting patterns. Experiment! One last hint regarding the use of a comb: make the frosting layer extra-thick, so you don't scrape down and expose the cake.

An easy way to decorate cakes is to press "goodies" onto the surface of the cake. Toasted hazelnuts, chopped pecans, chocolate jimmies (sprinkles or chocolate vermicelli), and shaved chocolate all work well and add to the flavor as well as the look of the finished cake. Consider pressing nuts on the sides of a cake and using a cake comb on the top. Squiggling melted chocolate in random patterns or fine parallel lines over the top adds a modern look, as does the use of cut stencils with sieved cocoa or powdered sugar.

# Appendix II
## *Miscellaneous Techniques*

### 1. Pan Preparation

Baking pans should be prepared in advance. Here are a few guidelines based on the types of pans and batters.

**a.** Batters which do not have butter, shortening, or oil in their recipes should have the sides of the pan coated with a thin film of vegetable shortening. Do not use butter as it will burn and darken the edge of the cake.

**b.** For *round or rectangular* cake pans, trace the outside bottom of the pan on parchment with a pencil and cut out the circle or rectangle. Place it in the bottom of the cake pan. If the batter is particularly stiff, a dab of shortening placed in the center of the pan before adding the parchment circle will prevent the liner from moving as the batter spreads.

**c.** For *half-sheet* pans (12-by-16-by-1-inch), measure the dimensions of the parchment by laying one corner of the parchment in the corner of the pan. Mark the length and width and cut to fit. Dab some shortening at the corners and in several rows in the middle of the pan and press the parchment to the pan.

**d.** For *springform* pans, cut a circle of parchment paper slightly larger than the bottom of the pan and cut several 2-inch strips of parchment. Dab the interior of the pan with vegetable shortening. Press the parchment circle to the bottom and line the sides with the strips. Be sure that all the strips overlap with each other and with the bottom circle.

### 2. Torting Layers

Slicing cake layers in half laterally is known as *torting*. Using a sharp, serrated, 10-inch knife, begin to slice the cake layer in half. Do not attempt to cut through the entire cake—just cut in an inch or so. Turn the cake and repeat, eventually making a cut all around the edge. Repeat, cutting in deeper this time. Be sure to keep the knife parallel to the work surface. Turn the cake as you make the third cut, and cut all the way through.

### 3. Fruit Preparation

a.   *Mangoes*. Peel the mango by cutting from end to end (across the long dimension of the fruit). Slice off the bottom quarter-inch so it will stand. Slice off each side by cutting in as close to the pit as possible. Trim the remaining flesh from the pit.

b.   *Peaches*. Peel the peach from the stem, down the sides, to the point (do not go around the circumference, as with an apple). Slice the bottom off so it will stand. Slice off each side by cutting down as close to the pit as possible. Trim the remaining flesh from the pit.

c.   *Apples*. Peel the apple by going around the circumference, from the stem to the blossom end. Cut the apple in half, from stem to blossom end through the core. For decorative slices, as required for a tart, core the halves by making a V cut to remove the core and seeds. Slice each half by making parallel cuts in the fruit. If the apple does not need to be cut decoratively, quarter each half, again cutting from stem to blossom end through the core. Cut out the core of each quarter by slicing parallel to the outside edge of the fruit. Slice each quarter to the thickness desired.

### 4. Removing Hazelnut Skins

Unless you can obtain hazelnuts that are already skinned, you will need to remove the outer, brown skin. Preheat your oven to 375°F, spread the hazelnuts on a half-sheet pan, and bake them until the skins are very dark and peeling away from the nut. Allow the nuts to cool and then rub them in a towel or in your hands to remove the skins. Chop or grind the nuts as directed.

### 5. Whipping Cream

Chill the mixing bowl and whip attachment thoroughly by placing them in a freezer for fifteen minutes. The cream should remain in the refrigerator until the operation begins. Put the cream in the bowl and start to beat on low speed. Gradually increase the mixing speed. When the whip first leaves a slight trail in the cream, add the sugar and continue to beat at medium speed. After a minute increase the speed to high and continue to beat until stiff. Scrape down the bowl and fold the mixture with a rubber spatula. Beat thirty seconds more. Use immediately or refrigerate.

# Appendix III
## *Recommended Equipment*

### Mixing

"Stand-alone" electric mixer with bowl 4-quarts or larger
Stainless steel and plastic bowls in graduated sizes
Rubber spatulas—reserved for baking only
Wire whips—small, medium, and large
Food processor
Blender

### Measuring

Scales—an ounce scale that measures to two pounds
Aluminum measuring cups (dry)—1 cup, 2 cup, 4 cup
Measuring cups (dry)—1/8, 1/4, 1/3, and 1/2 cup
Measuring spoons—1/8 teaspoon to 1 tablespoon
Clear plastic or glass measuring cups (liquid)—1 cup, 2 cup, 4 cup, 8 cup, graduated in fluid ounces

### Ovens

Gas or electric—calibrated and lined with ceramic tiles as explained in "Getting Started"
Microwave—variable power (double boiler can be substituted in most instances)

### Pastry

Large rolling pin
Pastry cloth
Pastry knife
Pastry scraper
Pastry bag—14-inch with plain, star, leaf, and rose tips
Metal spatulas for cake decoration, small and medium, straight and offset

Sifter
Pastry brushes—narrow, wide
Cake comb

## Knives

Paring
Chef's (8-inch)
Serrated (12-to-14-inch)

## Pots and pans

Heavy, nonreactive saucepans (such as stainless steel or enamelware)
   in assorted sizes
Double boiler
Four 9-inch round cake pans, nonstick preferred
Half-sheet rectangular baking pan (12-by-16-by-1-inch)
Square cake pan: 10-by-10-by-3 inches
One 10-inch springform pan—stainless steel if possible
One 10-inch tart pan with removable bottom
Pie pans—aluminum foil and Pyrex®
Rectangular baking dishes—Pyrex®, 2- and 3-quart
Small 7-inch loaf pan

## Miscellaneous

Cardboard cake boxes—10-by-10 inches, 1/2-inch and 2-inches deep
Cardboard cake circles—10-inch, 12-inch
Citrus juicer
Cutting boards—small and large, plastic
Parchment paper (available in the foil section of most supermarkets or
   where cake decorating equipment is sold)
Sieves
Thermometers: (1) oven, (2) immersion, (3) candy
Zester/grater